POCKET PUZZLES

Lillian Marcus is a major contributor to Starship, a page for children in the *Toronto Star*, from its inception in 1977 and is the author of several children's puzzle books. Her commissioned works include puzzles for both junior and adult publications, such as the Toronto Symphony Orchestra programme, the Ontario Science Centre newsletter and *OWL* magazine. She was the major contributor to Air Canada's *JETERAMA*, a puzzle book for young people.

Lillian's earlier experience is as an artist and fashion designer. Her writing career began after a trip to England. She picked up the 'In-flight' magazine to discover that there was no crossword puzzle. This started her on a new career, designing not only crossword puzzles but various kinds of word puzzles, for young and old alike.

POCKETFUL of PUZZLES

Lillian Marcus

Puffin Books

Puffin Books, Penguin Books Ltd, Harmondsworth, Middlesex, England
Viking Penguin Inc., 40 West 23rd Street, New York, New York 10010, U.S.A.
Penguin Books Australia Ltd, Ringwood, Victoria, Australia
Penguin Books Canada Ltd, 2801 John Street, Markham, Ontario, Canada L3R 1B4
Penguin Books (N.Z.) Ltd, 182-190 Wairau Road, Auckland 10, New Zealand

First published 1985

Copyright © Lillian Marcus, 1978, 1979, 1980, 1981, 1984
All rights reserved

Book and cover design by Vlasta van Kampen

Printed by Cox & Wyman Ltd, Reading

Canadian Cataloguing in Publication Data

Marcus, Lillian.
Pocketful of puzzles
ISBN 0 14 031750 3
1. Word games. 2. Puzzles. I. Title.
GV1507.W8M37 1984   793.73   C84-098142-2

Except in the United States of America,
this book is sold subject to the condition
that it shall not, by way of trade or otherwise,
be lent, re-sold, hired out, or otherwise circulated
without the publisher's prior consent in any form of
binding or cover other than that in which it is
published and without a similar condition
including this condition being imposed
on the subsequent purchaser

This book belongs to

Rachel E. Skeet.

CONTENTS

Crosswords	7
Centre Lines	50
Hidden Words	60
Secret Codes	70
This Way That Way	82
Boxwords	93
Anagrams	102
Solutions	109

Across

1. Holidays
8. Short for Charles
12. Go it alone
13. A tree
15. Insect
16. Resided
17. A Fish
18. Letter of the alphabet
19. Nasty
22. Part of a hospital
23. A direction (abbreviation)
24. A lot
25. Not full
27. Came together
28. Always
29. Thus
30. Part of the head

Down

2. Like
3. Frigid
4. Short for Albert
5. Toward
6. At no time
7. Slim
9. Relative of the rabbit
10. One
11. Small rock
14. Medical doctor (abbreviation)
16. Attorney
17. A mongrel
19. Charts
20. Some
21. Tardy
24. Pronoun (personal)
26. To pull

CROSSWORD

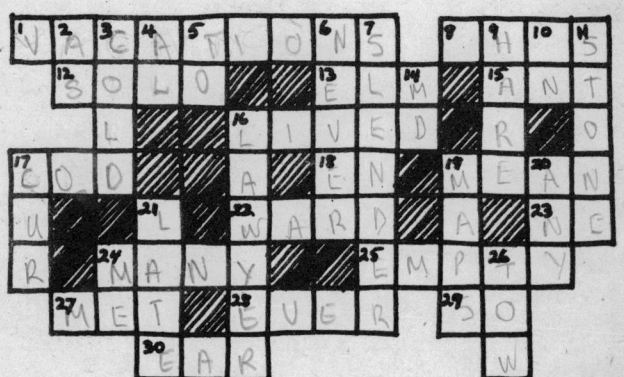

Across

1. To total
4. See this in the sky
6. Past
8. Got into a temper
10. A happening
13. A relative
14. A sleep sound
15. In addition
16. Unused
18. To snip
20. And (French)
22. Not as much
23. Gets bigger
24. Small poem
25. To pull along

Down

1. A mathematical snake?
2. Filth
3. A running game
4. A fish
5. Unclosed
7. Jewel
8. A part in a play
9. Reply
11. Said out loud
12. Birds' homes
13. _ _ _ _ castles
17. Part of a sailing ship
19. Employs
21. Part of the foot
22. Not high

CROSSWORD 2

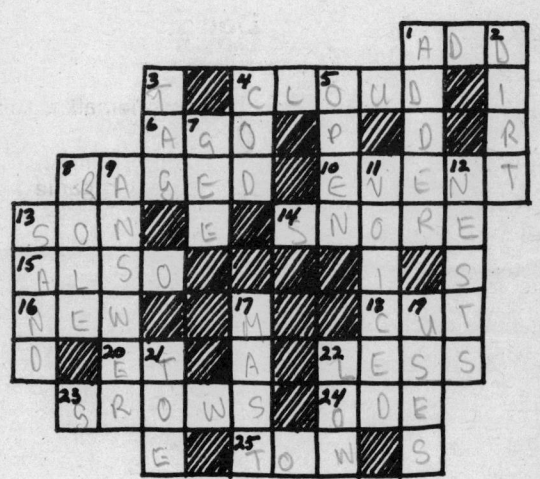

Why did the teacher wear dark glasses?

Because her class was so bright!

Across

1. Opposite of succeeding
6. South Dakota (abbreviation)
8. Mexican pancake
9. Had a meal
10. 'The' in Spanish
11. Indefinite article
14. To make unhappy
17. Hurry
20. Metal
21. Damp
22. Small number

Down

1. A language
2. Neuter pronoun
3. 6th note of the musical scale
4. Frozen water
5. Negative reply
6. Not as fresh
7. A cave
12. Desired
13. Like
14. Viewed
15. Cooing bird
16. North east (abbreviation)
18. Grow old
19. A pair

What did the absent-minded skunk say when the wind changed direction?

„·ʍou ǝɯ oʇ ʞɔɐq ɓuᴉɯoɔ ll,ɐ s,ʇI„

CROSSWORD 3

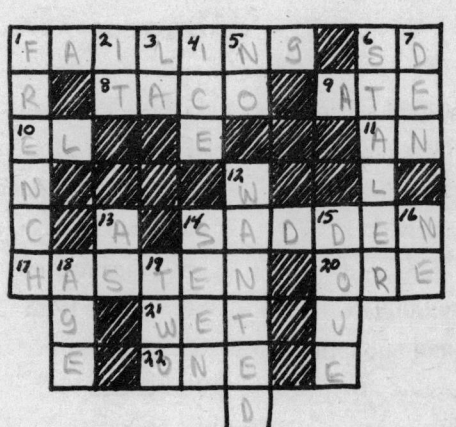

Across

1. Completed
6. A baby bear
8. A feline
9. A short sleep
11. Headed
13. A tiny drink
14. Sun god
15. College degree
16. Untidy
19. To throw
20. A style of car
21. Tumbled
24. To challenge
25. The (French)
26. Unused
27. The (Spanish)

Down

1. Fish have them
2. Pinched
3. Science (abbr.)
4. Having lots of hair
5. And (French)
6. Soothes
7. A place to sleep
10. Pointed
12. To loosen
17. The devil
18. Made a snoring sound
19. Higher
22. Church seat
23. Snakelike fish

CROSSWORD

★ · ★ · ★ · ★ · ★ · ★ · ★ 4

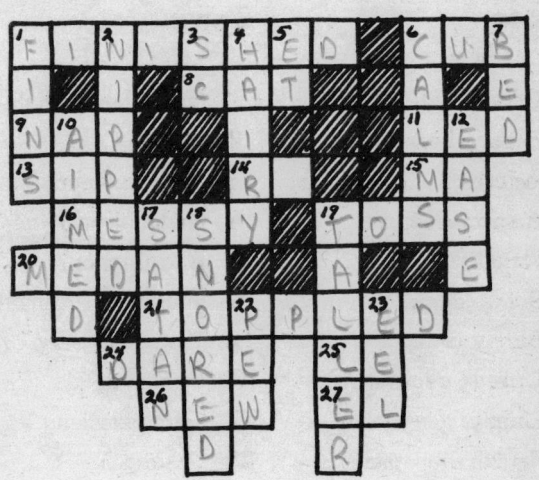

Why did the miser put all his money under the mattress?

He wanted something to fall back on!

Across

1. Admonishes
6. Exclamation
8. Ice cream _ _ _ _
9. A species of tree
11. An alternative
12. Dens
13. Alright (slang)
14. Edna North (initials)
15. Long playing (abbr.)
17. Part of a hospital
18. Father
19. Part of the head
21. A feline
22. Lion talk
23. Knockout (abbr.)
24. Look after

Down

1. Short handled shovel
2. A bottle top
3. Upon
4. The (French)
5. Thin
7. Musical instrument
9. Always
10. Feminine title
12. Person lacking bravery
15. A songbird
16. Tardy
18. Tap lightly
20. Weep

CROSSWORD

★ · ★ · ★ · ★ · ★ · ★ · ★ 5

What happens to old refrigerators?

They lose their cool!

Across

1. A vow
3. Exclamation
5. A negative
6. Very warm
7. Like
8. Frozen water
9. Belonging to it
12. Dip into liquid
13. A green vegetable
14. Morning moisture
16. Robert Orwood's initials
17. Part of the face
18. Seasoning
21. Glide on ice

Down

1. Placards
2. Medical doctor (abbr.)
3. A winter sport
4. Consumed
5. Part of the finger
6. To keep back
10. Halt
11. Rapid
12. A cave
15. Plural pronoun
19. Exists
20. Each (abbr.)

CROSSWORD

★ · ★ · ★ · ★ · ★ · ★ · ★ · 6

Why is a goose like a car?

They both honk.

Across

2. Wild animal
5. Another wild animal
7. Alternative
8. He (French)
9. Personal pronoun
10. Father
11. Writing fluid
12. Exists
13. To correct
15. Part of a barbecue
18. Long playing (abbr.)
19. Kind of tree
21. Ontario (abbr.)
22. More than one
25. North east (abbr.)
26. Require
27. Male honey bees
30. At this time

Down

1. Cutting tools
2. Stomach pains
3. Metal
4. Antlered animals
6. Left out
7. A birth stone
11. Inactive
14. At no time
16. Long sticks
17. Within
20. Male title (abbr.)
23. To finish
24. Afresh
28. Upon
29. A negative

CROSSWORD 7

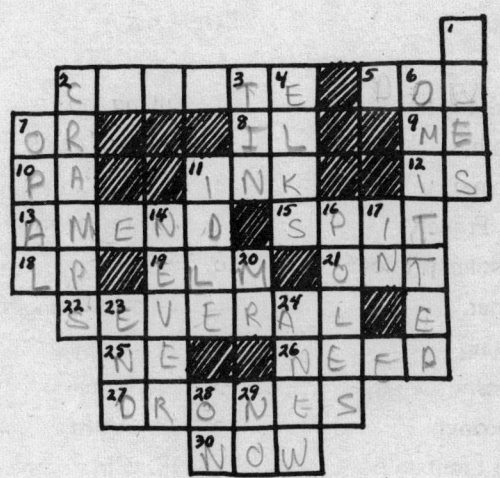

What did one tonsil say to the other tonsil?

"Let's get ready. The doctor's taking us out!"

Across

2. Melodious sounds
6. To poke
8. Water barrier
10. Meat
12. Challenge
13. Cylinder
14. To fib
15. 2nd note of the musical scale
16. To stain
17. A rodent
19. Editor (abbr.)
21. Poultry products
23. Spring holiday
26. Right away
27. A flower
28. Road (abbr.)

Down

1. A bunny
3. Above
4. Girl's name
5. Rabbit food
7. Stinging insect
9. Come together
11. Blooms
12. Pattern
13. A trio
18. Girl's name
20. A celebrity
22. Female pig
24. Spanish (abbr.)
25. To finish

CROSSWORD

★·★·★·★·★·★·★ 8

Across

6. Storage places
8. Like
10. A large sign
11. Gone
12. Edge
13. Belonging to
14. South Africa (abbr.)
16. Summed up
19. Goes out
21. A kind of boat
22. A kind of rock
23. Saint (abbr.)
25. Twisted

Down

1. Established (abbr.)
2. Weird
3. A snake
4. Fuel
5. Top of a house
7. Pronoun
9. Firm
13. To unlock
14. Waited upon
15. Belonging to it
16. Later
17. River in Scotland
18. Doctor (abbr.)
20. Narrow opening
23. Science (abbr.)
24. Toward

CROSSWORD

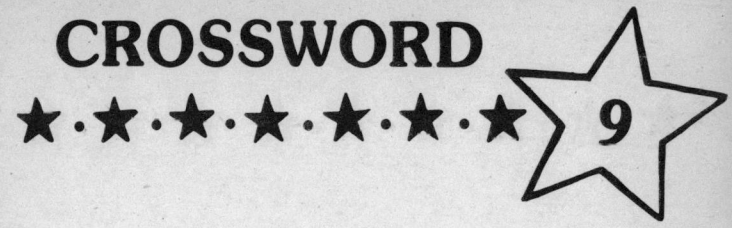

9

Why couldn't the elephants go swimming together?

They only had one pair of trunks between them.

Across

1. Berates
6. Eastern ruler
10. A conical shape
11. A citrus fruit
12. An alternative
13. A grown-up kitten
15. Upon
16. A short poem
17. Long playing (abbr.)
19. To carry on the body
21. Father
22. Part of the head
23. Obese
24. To peruse
27. Soft and gentle
29. Smooth

Down

1. A ladle
2. A vegetable
3. Upon
4. The (French)
5. A colour tone
6. Slang (abbr.)
7. A friendly greeting
8. Part of the verb 'To be'
9. Assist
13. They aren't brave at all!
14. A beverage
17. A song bird
18. Tardy
20. A colour
21. To tap lightly
25. A snakelike fish
26. Part of the verb 'To be'
28. All right (slang)

CROSSWORD ★·★·★·★·★·★·★ 10

What has arms but can't raise them?

A chair, of course!

Across

1. Trousers
6. Fruit
10. Not shallow
11. Unhappy
12. Editor (abbr.)
13. A small number
15. 2,000 pounds
16. The (Spanish)
18. A black bird
21. A garbage place
23. Whirl
25. A pole
27. Self
28. Not high
29. Reply

Down

2. Snakes
3. A direction (abbr.)
4. Thomas Edison (initials)
5. To stain
6. A road
7. Postscript (abbr.)
8. Tardy
9. Edward (abbr.)
14. Move the head in greeting
17. A cover
19. To unlock
20. False hair pieces
22. Professional (abbr.)
24. Immediately
26. Night bird

CROSSWORD
★・★・★・★・★・★・ 11

Across

3. All over the place
8. Snakelike fish
9. Large fowl
11. A triple
15. An exit
18. He (French)
20. To soar
21. Go by
23. Blacksmith's tool
25. The first lady
26. Riding gear
28. Boating

Down

1. Tempo
2. Fright
4. Pronoun (plural)
5. Pronoun (singular)
6. Gnome
7. Poultry product
10. A school subject
12. Hoola _ _ _ _
13. Part of the head
14. To exist
16. Horse feed
17. Tumbles
19. Full of pep
22. Unhappy
24. The (French)
27. Consume

CROSSWORD 12

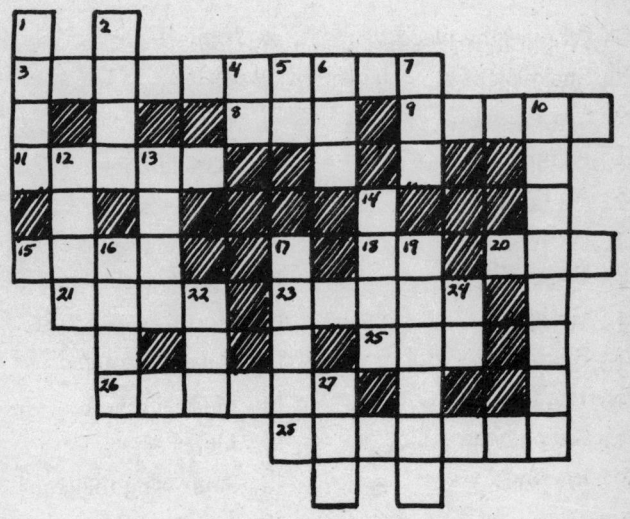

How did Jane lose her alarm clock?

It just went off while she was asleep!

Across

1. Night flying mammal
4. Advertisements (abbr.)
7. Atmosphere
9. A hidden entry
11. A faucet
12. A cave
13. Including
14. Created
15. Tree juice
16. Frosted
17. Fits
21. A beast
22. Part of the head
23. A church service
25. Put out money

Down

2. Join
3. To swap
4. To total
5. Female deer
6. Male offspring
7. A boring tool
8. Rebellions
10. Imitated
13. Fruit
14. Musical note
17. Identical
18. A growing thing
19. 6th note of the musical sc
20. Senior (abbr.)
24. Saint (abbr.)

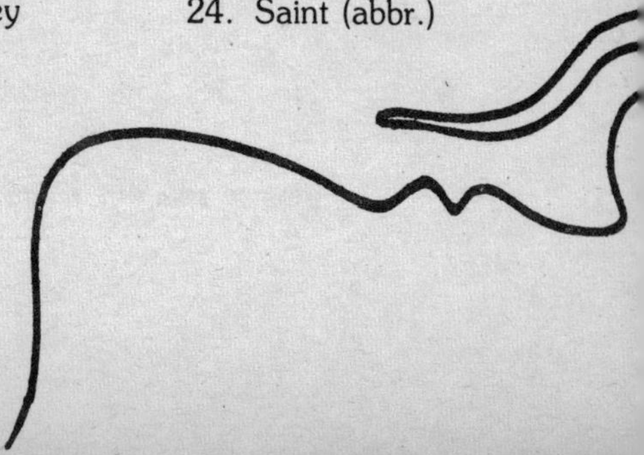

CROSSWORD 13

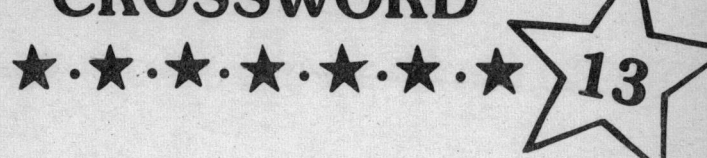

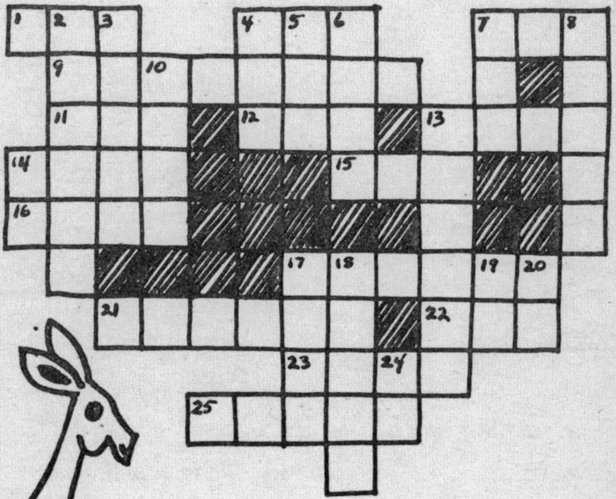

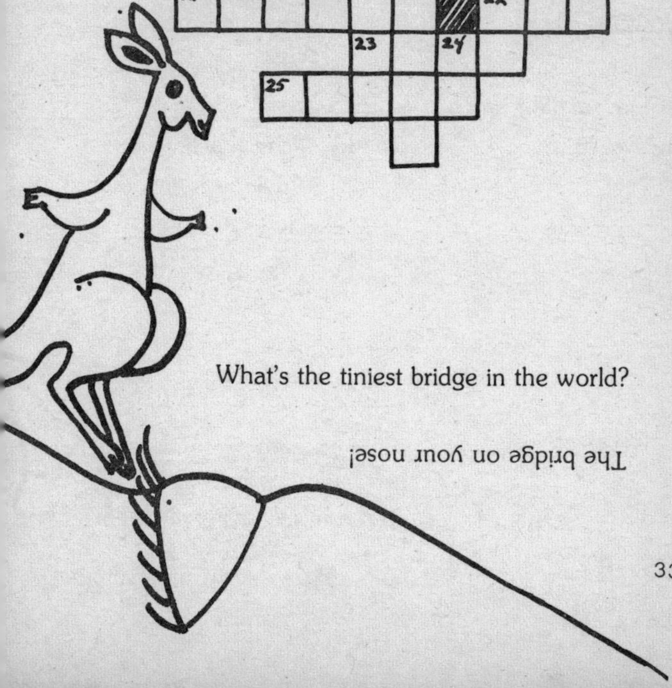

What's the tiniest bridge in the world?

The bridge on your nose!

Across

3. A fuel
6. A writing table
8. A type of steak
9. Octopus's arms and legs
11. Biblical garden
12. Thus
14. Girl's name
18. Graven images
19. The smallest amount
20. Tree juice

Down

1. Totalled
2. Flowers
3. Gustave (abbr.)
4. Before noon (abbr.)
5. An extra
7. Kenneth (abbr.)
8. Restrain
10. Vegetable
13. Night bird
14. Mine (Italian)
15. Advertisements (abbr.)
16. He (French)
17. Energy

What did the ringmaster say to the misbehaving elephant?

Pack your trunk and get out!

CROSSWORD 14

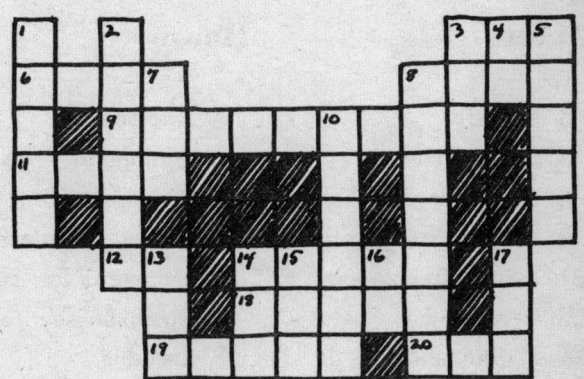

Across

1. On high
3. Spelling (abbr.)
5. A season
7. A seasoning
10. Pointed
11. Chief male character
13. In addition
16. To interfere
19. Magnificent
21. A colour
22. Cat sound
23. Father
24. Periods
25. Demonstrate

Down

1. Employ
2. Young dog
3. Smudged
4. A punctuation mark
6. Member of Parliament (abbr.)
8. Got better
9. Relate
12. Muslim rulers
13. Mimicked
14. September (abbr.)
15. A burden
17. To sketch
18. Editor (abbr.)
20. Doctor (abbr.)
23. Perform

CROSSWORD
★·★·★·★·★·★·★ 15

When is a girl's dress like a frog?

When it's a jumper!

Across

1. To battle
4. Form
9. Tiny bits
10. A march
12. Behold
14. A single
15. Chartered accountant (abbr.)
16. No trump (abbr.)
17. Above
18. Banners
21. An appointment
23. Come together
24. Not bright
25. Year (abbr.)
26. A title
27. Retained

Down

1. Silver colored paper
2. An opening
3. A large crowd
4. To take one's part
5. Garden tool
6. By
7. Father
8. To get away
11. Insects
13. To present
15. To slice
19. The (French)
20. Dined
21. Filth
22. Morning (abbr.)
23. Belonging to me
24. To dunk
26. South east (abbr.)

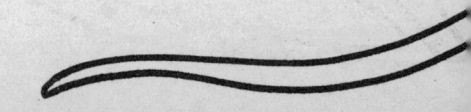

CROSSWORD
★·★·★·★·★·★·★ 16

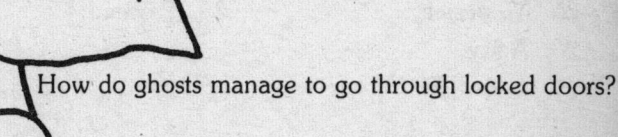

How do ghosts manage to go through locked doors?

They all have skeleton keys.

★·★·★·★·★·★·★·★·★·★

Across

1. Carrot-loving animals
6. Large pig
7. To ponder
9. Short poem
10. Mischievous one
13. Gorilla
14. Above
15. Andrew (abbr.)
16. To cut
18. An elm
19. Owned
21. An alternative
23. A tramp
24. To pester
26. A sign or portent

Down

1. A rat
2. Grow older
3. Neuter pronoun
4. Opposite of here
5. Yes (Spanish)
6. Jumps
8. Domain
11. Medical doctor (abbr.)
12. A snake
14. Musical composition
17. To press
20. Exclamation
22. A single
25. Proceed

Do you know why Mary married the janitor?

He swept her off her feet!

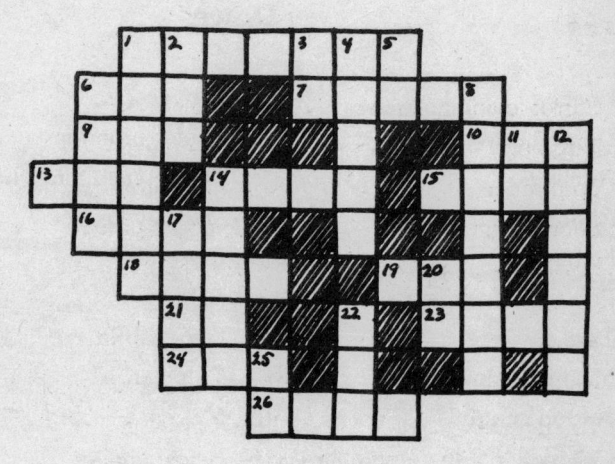

CROSSWORD

★·★·★·★·★·★·★· 17

Across

1. Boating
7. Domesticated
8. A tabby
10. Rhode Island (abbr.)
11. Father
12. Public relations (abbr.)
13. Title
17. Male offspring (plural)
19. A food centre
21. Occupational therapy (abbr.)
22. Short for Emma
23. Masculine pronoun
24. To loosen
26. Thought about
28. A kind

Down

1. Shrivelled
2. Neuter pronoun
3. The (French feminine)
4. Mischievous one
5. Close by
6. A chart
9. Had faith in
14. To point
15. Mountain (abbr.)
16. Reverberation
17. Unpleasant facial expressi
18. Part of the face
20. Chickens
25. Short for Arthur
26. Father
27. Perform

CRISSCROSS ★·★·★·★·★·★·★ 18

Why did Johnny lock his dad in the fridge?

Because he wanted cold pop!

Across

1. Sweet liquid
3. Later
5. Donkey
7. New Brunswick (abbr.)
9. A small bite
10. Plates
13. To steal
16. A melody
17. Transmission of sound
18. Yard (abbr.)
19. A royal female
21. A direction
22. 365 days
26. A Wonderland character
28. To cook
29. Opposite of even

Down

1. A day of the week
2. Part of a window
3. A snake
4. Cowboy gatherings
6. Short for sister
8. A robin
11. 'Yes' in Spanish
12. Joyful
13. A small nail
14. A fruit drink
15. A loving gesture
17. Registered nurse (abbr.)
20. European country
23. Part of the head
24. Rhode Island (abbr.)
25. A colour
27. Company (abbr.)

CROSSWORD

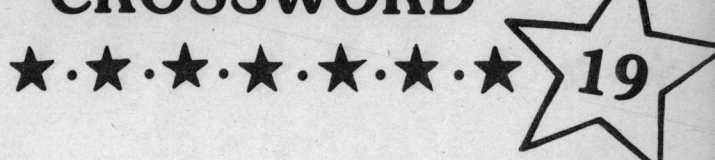

★ · ★ · ★ · ★ · ★ · ★ · ★ **19**

Across

1. Stain
5. Heavenly body
6. Begin
10. Beneath
12. Upon
13. Exists
14. A number
15. 7th note of the musical scale
16. Father
17. Sky formation
19. Top of a sore
22. Capital of Norway
23. From Denmark
25. Part of the head
28. Less expensive
29. A limb

Down

1. A relative
2. Pea container
3. A single
4. Hour (abbr.)
5. Melodious sounds
7. Toward
8. Absurd actions
9. Metal
11. A thoroughfare
13. Neuter pronoun
16. To chastise
18. A burden
19. Thus
20. Albert (abbr.)
21. A watercraft
24. To get better
26. Gorilla
27. Reginald (abbr.)

CROSSWORD

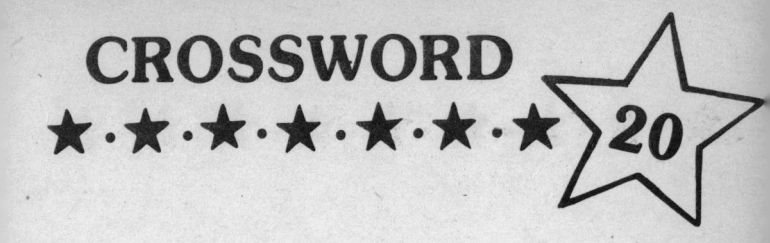

★ · ★ · ★ · ★ · ★ · ★ · ★ **20**

Where should you put your underwear when you travel?

In your briefcase, naturally!

★·★·★·★·★·★·★·★·★

Across

1. Insects
7. A radio frequency
9. Fastened
11. A beverage
12. Doctor (abbr.)
13. Sound of hesitation
14. Feminine pronoun
15. Animal found in Australia
19. Require
21. By
23. Katherine (abbr.)
24. Like
26. Plural of 'be'
27. Liquid flows

Down

2. Finish
3. Roofing material
4. 51 in Roman numerals
5. The (Spanish)
6. Use your eyes
7. A charge
8. Selling place
10. Arid
11. Ponder
16. Soft drinks
17. Equipment
18. Rowing equipment
20. Part of the head
22. French pronoun
25. South east (abbr.)
26. Before noon (abbr.)

CRISSCROSS 21

Instructions:
Write the answer to each clue in the space beside it. When you've filled in all the answers, you'll be able to read down the *centre line*.

50

CENTRE LINE

★ · ★ · ★ · ★ · ★ · ★ · **1**

Clue	Answer		Clue
Not as much	L E S S		
	T A X I		Public vehicle
Cans	T I N S		
	B E N T		Crooked
Jungle animal	L I O N		
	L I C E		Vermin
Create	M A K E		
	M I N I		Opposite of maxi
Ill	S I C K		
	P A S S		Go by
Fog	M I S T		
	M E N U		Bill of fare
Level	F L A T		
	D E A F		Non-hearing
Finishes	E N D S		
	T I N T		To colour

CENTRE LINE 2

Clue	Answer
Liberate	F _ _ _
T A X I	Public vehicle
Slim	T H I N
Mountains	A L P S
P A S S	Go by
Capable	A B L E
C A L F	Baby cow
Inactive	I D L E
M E N D	Repair
Profound	D _ _ _
P U L L	Tug
Consumes	E A T S

Why do bees have such sticky hairs?

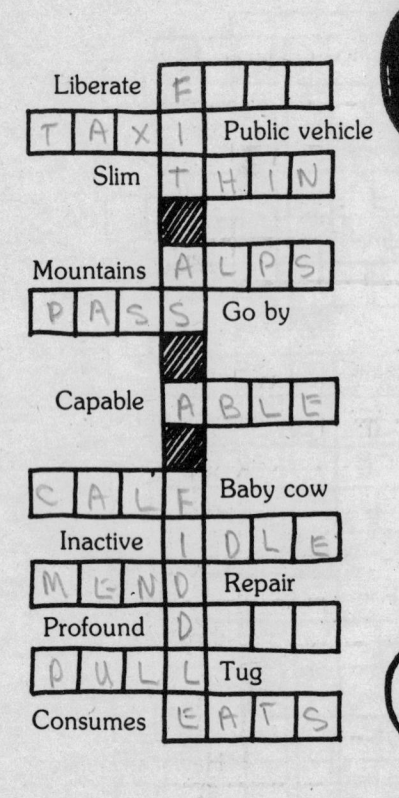

Because they have honey combs!

CENTRE LINE

3

M	A	T	E	Pal
Capable	A	B	L	E
				Brash

Pain — A C H E
L E T S — Allows

Insects — ☐☐☐☐

☐☐☐☐ — Shape
Friend — ☐☐☐☐
☐☐☐☐ — To teem
Sliver — ☐☐☐☐
R I C H — Wealthy

Assist — H E L P
☐☐☐☐ — Hawaiian dance
To relax — ☐☐☐☐
☐☐☐☐ — To own

CENTRE LINE

★·★·★·★·★·★·★· 4

Adhesive

Not any

Tidy

Ago

Wild animal

Destiny

Boring tools

Pots

Grows older

Tumble

Insects

Shape

Infant

CENTRE LINE

★·★·★·★·★·★·★· 5

- Not fast
- To hurt
- Gorillas
- 60 minutes
- To rip
- Hawaiian dance
- Rescue
- A bean
- Labour
- To dart
- Frosts
- Halt

Why did the composer spend so much time in bed?

Because he liked writing sheet music!

CENTRE LINE

★·★·★·★·★·★·★· 6

- ____ Metal
- Above ____
- ____ Black bird
- A colour ____
- ____ A sport
- Holler ____
- ____ Pots
- Helps ____
- ____ Ache
- Moist ____
- ____ Public vehicle
- ____ Pleasant ____
- ____ Hairless
- Small island ____
- ____ Musical instrument
- Part of the face ____
- ____ Fastens

56

CENTRE LINE

★·★·★·★·★·★·★· 7

- Go by
- A direction
- Rescue
- Simple
- Crooked
- Pain
- Is seated
- Identical
- Bill of fare
- Got bigger
- Mother
- To hurry

How do you keep a rhinoceros from charging?

Take away his credit card!

CENTRE LINE

★ · ★ · ★ · ★ · ★ · ★ · ★ · 8

Part of the face
Rip
Ventilates
Famous canal
Shout
Latin country
Remain
On the ocean
Whip
Dog's name
Above
Midday

Why are playing cards like wolves?

Because they come in packs!

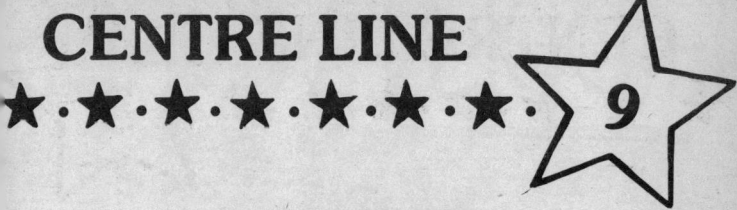

CENTRE LINE

★·★·★·★·★·★·★· 9

- Not early
- Opposite to maxi
- Precious metal
- Dart
- Cans
- A continent
- To halt
- Hawaiian dance
- Liberate
- Detest
- And
- Trial
- Make hot
- Donated
- The balance

HIDDEN WORDS

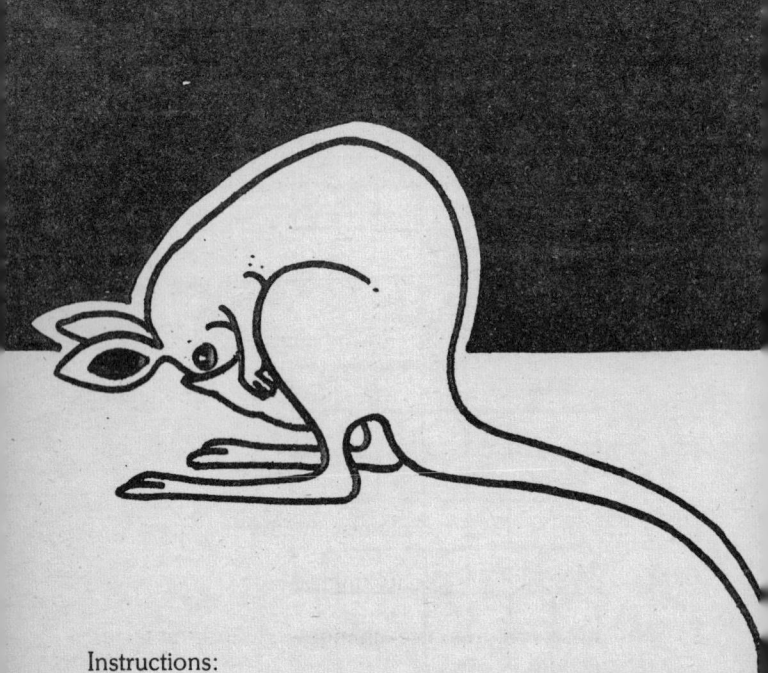

Instructions:
Look through each sentence to find the hidden word.
Example: Wild animals can <u>be a</u> real menace.

60

HIDDEN WORDS
Animals

★ · ★ · ★ · ★ · ★ · ★ · ★ · ★ · ★

1. They eat slop, I guess, every day. Pig

2. They are a real prize, brave and colourful. zebra

3. Felines make strange music at times. cat

4. Do explain why these dainty creatures are so shy. Doe

5. Rabbits rarely share their food. hare

6. They have a keen sense of smell but have made errors in judgment. deer

7. Jack assists us with the jobs on the farm. Jackass

8. If oxen could transport us we would use less energy. fox

9. They might sleep under a tree limb at night. bat

10. This creature is neither drab, biting nor bold. rabbit

11. A pup or cup in each case ends in the same letters. porcupine

12. They could trim oleander bush roots and pile them all over the lawn. Mole

13. This animal is not terribly fast on land. otter

14. Leo pardoned the spotty jungle beast. Leopard

15. No transfer returns or exchanges will find the fastest rat-catcher. Ferret

16. There are many varieties of these well-known sheep. ewe

HIDDEN WORDS
Insects
★ · ★ · ★ · ★ · ★ · ★ · ★ · ★

1. Beth or Nettie will babysit tonight.
2. Look at that jello. It set seconds after I mixed it.
3. We could call Joan tomorrow.
4. Please show a special interest in these insect pictures.
5. Standing beside Babe Evelyn looks quite tiny.
6. Where does he get off lying like that?

Birds

1. One rarely finds these birds near the St. Lawrence market.
2. These birds have been known to wheel right around in a circle.
3. Listening to a beautiful oratorio leaves me comparing the voices to the song of the birds.
4. This bird measures about seven and a half inches in length.
5. We saw hundreds of these birds as we drove past Arlington Street.
6. They sing with a throb in their throats.
7. Those two birds both rushed into the bird bath together.
8. They seem to spar, rotating about for ages.

HIDDEN WORDS
Names

★ · ★ · ★ · ★ · ★ · ★ · ★ · ★ · ★

1. The cane I loaned was never returned.
2. That sale on Monday sounds interesting.
3. Did Ann yell or did I imagine it?
4. The metal I cemented fell apart.
5. Such drivel is exasperating.
6. Diet helped me to lose weight.
7. Tantrums and rages are upsetting.
8. We had to rush Ann on to the stage.
9. We'd like to meet a marathon entrant.
10. Jean can always be found working energetically.
11. Do ugly ducklings grow up to be beautiful?
12. We hope terns never become extinct.
13. Bevels are necessary in carpentry.
14. Bart hurried hoping he would not be late for school.

HIDDEN WORDS
Summer

★ · ★ · ★ · ★ · ★ · ★ · ★ · ★

1. That chant sounds Arabian.

2. Albert entertained his friends at summer camp.

3. That ceiling, if lowered, would make the rooms hot in summer.

4. This sort of music, amplified, nearly breaks my eardrums.

5. The softest sand I've ever walked on was almost white.

6. Will a kennel fit on our small back porch?

7. Bess and May have gone on holiday.

Winter

1. This hovel is a filthy mess.

2. It's Dad's car for me when I'm older.

3. It's now, Ma, not tomorrow when I need the car.

4. I bought that mask at Esme's store.

5. Bob bets we ate Ron's candy.

6. She told us to steam it ten seconds and then drain it.

7. John was a star in Kingston years ago.

HIDDEN WORDS
Vehicles
★ · ★ · ★ · ★ · ★ · ★ · ★ · ★

1. The last rail eroded as the train track could not be used.
2. A cab usually cruises downtown.
3. There had been gin, early on, in that bottle.
4. The basic arsonist cannot resist fires.
5. Music, art and literature enrich everyone.
6. I saw a gondola, not a boat.

Watercraft

1. I'll go into the water after I do my homework.
2. That feather boa tickles.
3. I gave Erica no eats at all.
4. I can say, "Achtung". It means "Attention" in German.
5. The dish I picked out matched my set.
6. I prefer rye bread to white bread.
7. Ask if Frank will be home after school.

HIDDEN WORDS
Fires

★ · ★ · ★ · ★ · ★ · ★ · ★ · ★ · ★

1. Has Irene gone out again?

2. He gave that saw a terrific hug.

3. What is the attraction over there?

4. Janie's cape is hand-knitted.

5. We're glad Dervishes are fully explained in our new book.

6. When Dad had flu, he shivered and shook.

7. There are many trees such as pine, ash, elm et cetera in the forest.

Carpentry

1. This awl is a bit clumsy. saw

2. Is the Dr. ill too? Drill

3. A sudden ailment kept our guest away.

4. Max excelled in diving at school. nail

5. All adders are dangerous. Axe / ladder

6. This plan establishes our future direction. plane

7. Is Les having some people in to help him? shavings

HIDDEN WORDS
Flavours

★ · ★ · ★ · ★ · ★ · ★ · ★ · ★ · ★

1. Let's give this car a melon-coloured paint job.
2. If you get in the van, I'll arrange everything.
3. This salmon does taste good. Almond
4. Jack puts his little monkey in a cage at night.
5. Will I meet some of your friends at the party?
6. My uncle has a super farm in Trenton.
7. Is it garlic or ice bags that will cure a headache?

Desserts

1. The soup I especially like is mushroom. Pies
2. We bought Eric a keg of nails for his birthday. cake
3. That story about Art seems far-fetched. tart
4. We fed the ape a chicken sandwich. peach
5. I love licorice, cream and fruit for dessert. ice cream
6. We call Tom Marcus 'Tardy Tom' because he is always late. custard
7. It takes jam a long time to jell on humid days. jello

HIDDEN WORDS
Relatives

★ · ★ · ★ · ★ · ★ · ★ · ★ · ★

1. I thought it was a puma until I noticed the stripes.
2. A noun clearly is a thing.
3. Glass is terribly fragile.
4. Connie certainly is good-looking!
5. I left my scarf at her house.
6. Will the chemicals at the lab rot her finger nails?
7. Viv likes any jam other than peach.

Vegetables

1. That car rotates on a block.
2. At noon I only have half an hour to spare for lunch.
3. That auto mat offers lots of protection.
4. That urn I put there looks just right.
5. Lee keeps rabbits in her back yard.
6. He must be ethical in every way.
7. Give that tape a second try.

HIDDEN WORDS
Back to School

★ · ★ · ★ · ★ · ★ · ★ · ★ · ★ · ★

1. I just ate a cherry which was delicious.
2. Hold on to the bicycle handles, son.
3. If you lift the cup up, I'll pour the milk.
4. Which Al keeps the blackboards clean?
5. We built a very wide skating rink.
6. Vera served us all lemonade.
7. That collar gives our pup a pert look.

Ailments

1. You must think of me as less than perfect.
2. I tell you, Mum, psychology is my best subject.
3. This topic, old hat as it is, will be just right.
4. If Luke calls me tell him I'll be back soon.
5. If Vi rushes she will just make the concert.
6. On John's head a cheap hat doesn't look cheap!
7. Luckily we were near a checkout counter.

Secret Codes

Instructions:
Each symbol on these pages stands for a letter of the alphabet.
Crack the code by figuring out *which* letters the symbols represent.
When you're finished, you'll have a list of words that all have something to do with the title heading at the top of the page.

SECRET CODES
Colours

★ · ★ · ★ · ★ · ★ · ★ · ★ · ★ · ★ · ★

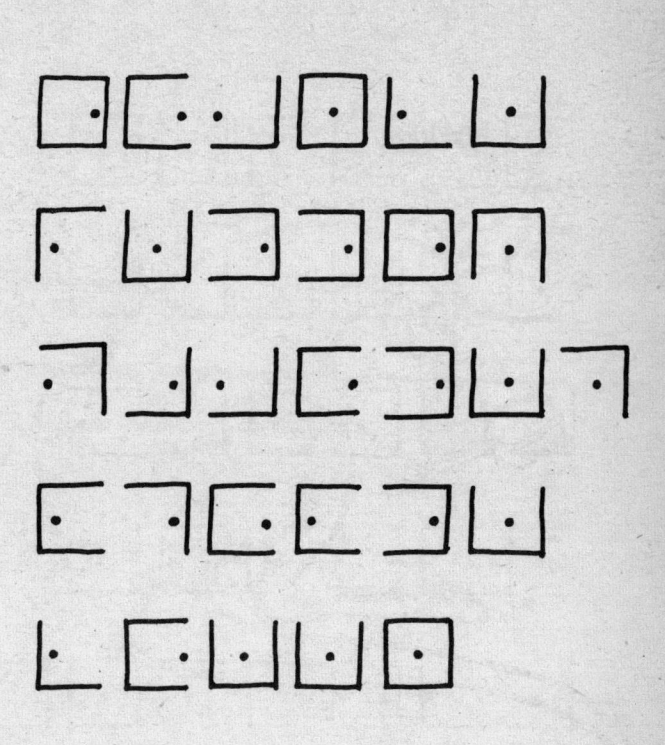

What does an envelope say when you lick it?

Nothing. It just shuts up!

SECRET CODES
Pets

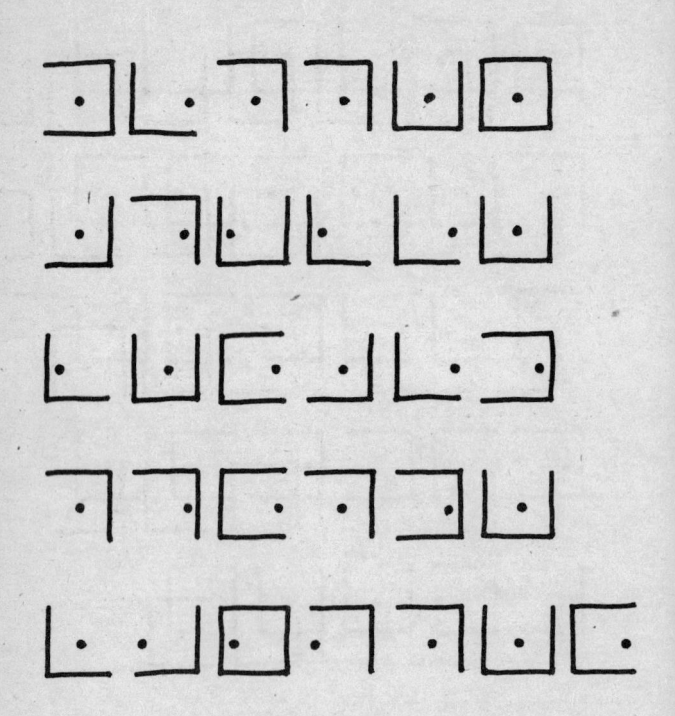

★ • ★ • ★ • ★ • ★ • ★ • ★ • ★

What works when it plays and plays when it works?

A fountain, of course!

SECRET CODES
Languages

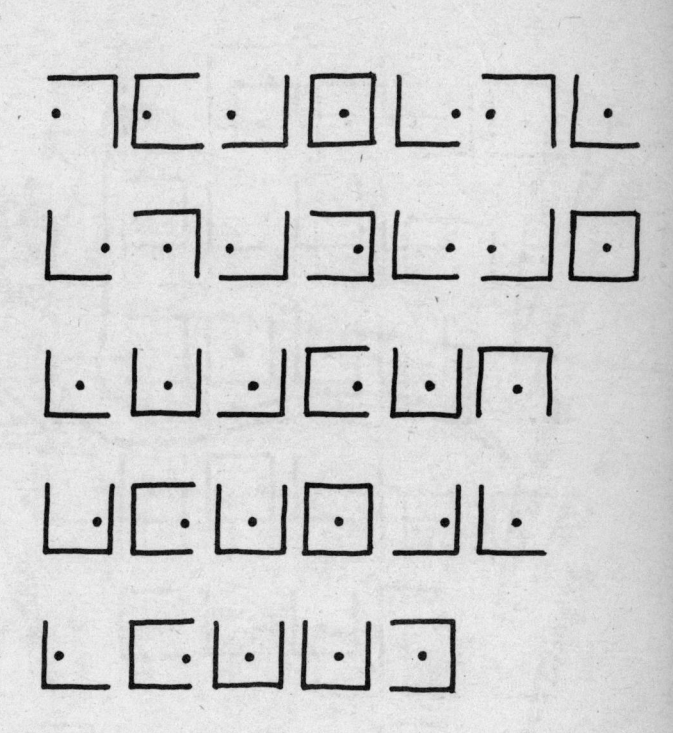

★ · ★ · ★ · ★ · ★ · ★ · ★ · ★ · ★

When is an elevator disappointing?

When it lets you down!

SECRET CODES
Animals

★ · ★ · ★ · ★ · ★ · ★ · ★ · ★ · ★ · ★ · ★

Do you know how to make gold soup?

Simple! Just put fourteen *carrots* in it!

SECRET CODES
Birds

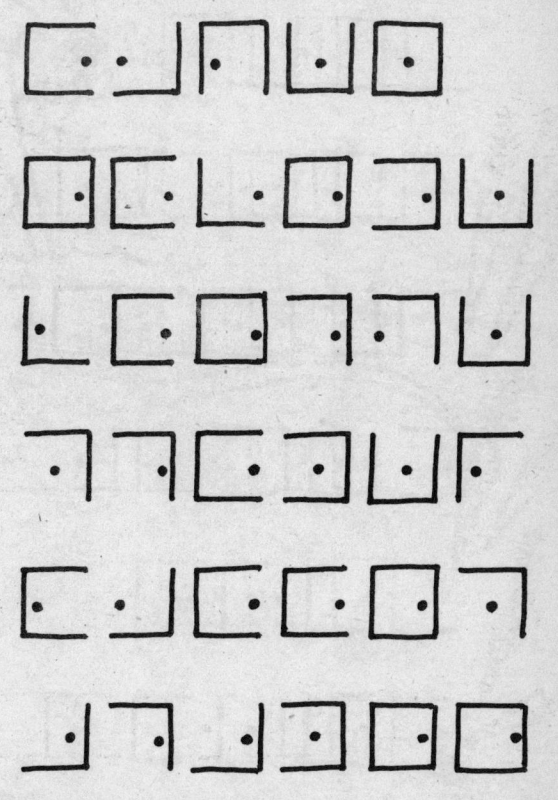

★ • ★ • ★ • ★ • ★ • ★ • ★ • ★ • ★

What starts with an E and ends with an E and contains one letter?

An envelope.

SECRET CODES
Swimming Creatures

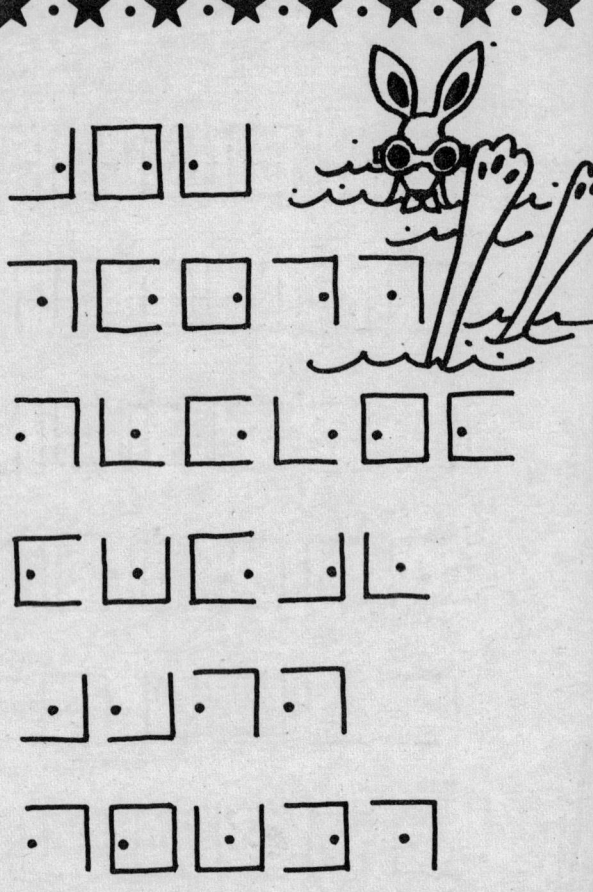

★ · ★ · ★ · ★ · ★ · ★ · ★ · ★ · ★ · ★

SECRET CODES
Pictures
★ · ★ · ★ · ★ · ★ · ★ · ★ · ★ · ★

SECRET CODES
Drawing Supplies

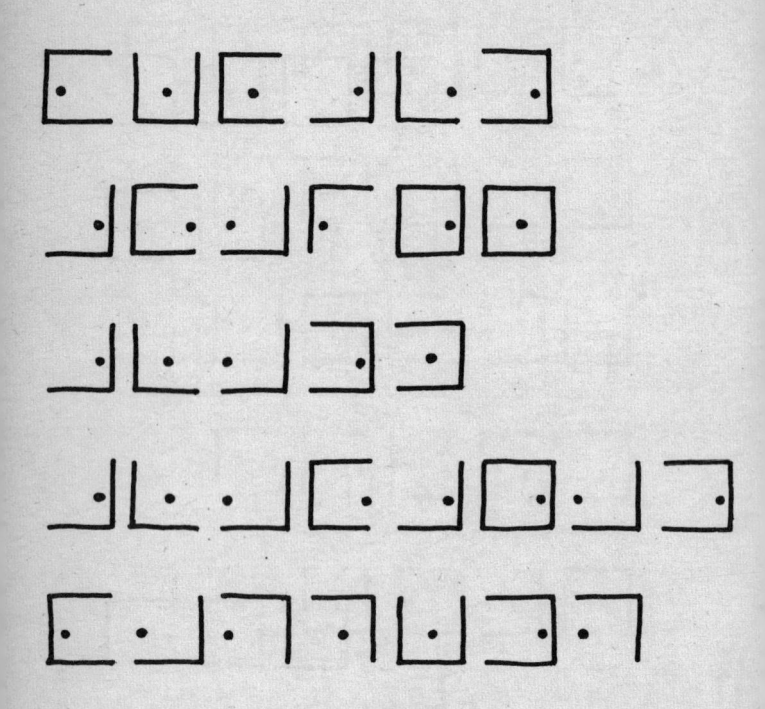

★ · ★ · ★ · ★ · ★ · ★ · ★ · ★ · ★

Which nut can you hang a picture on?

A walnut, of course!

SECRET CODES
Tools
★·★·★·★·★·★·★·★·★·★

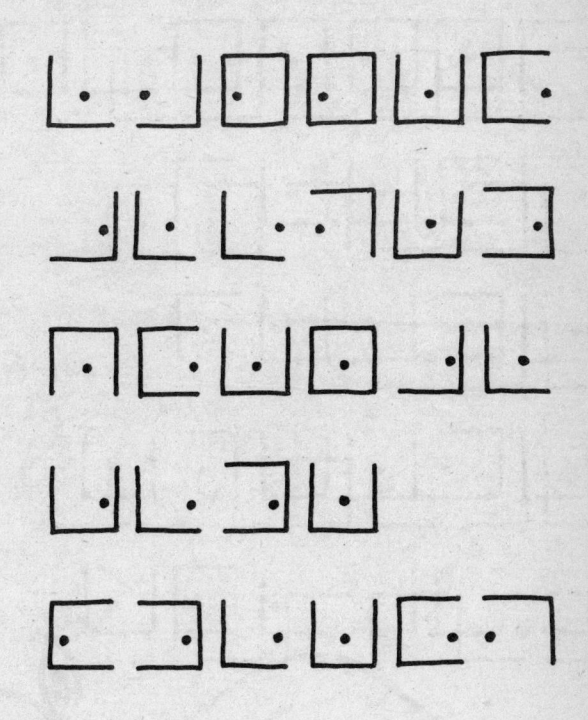

Who always gets paid for never doing a day's work?

A night watchman

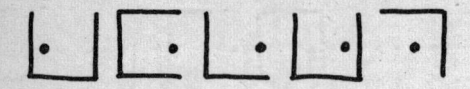

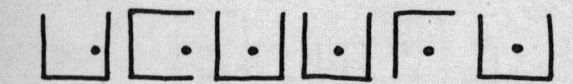

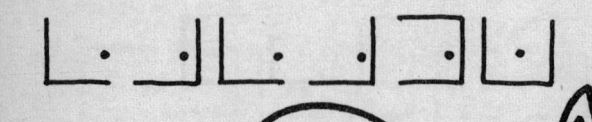

SECRET CODES
Winter

★·★·★·★·★·★·★·★·★·★

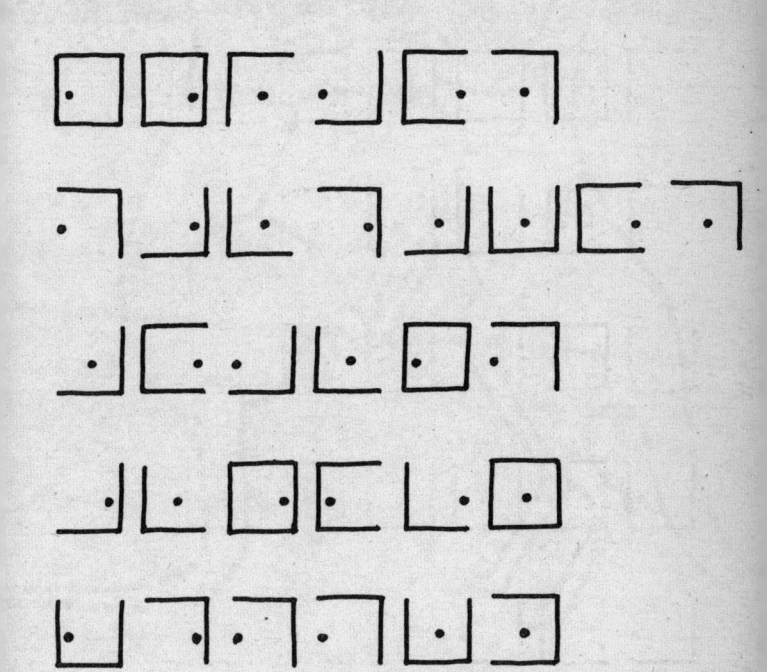

SECRET CODES
Composers
★·★·★·★·★·★·★·★·★

THIS WAY   THAT WAY

Instructions:
Fill in the squares as if they were crossword puzzles. When each square is complete, it should read the same down as it does across.

THIS WAY THAT WAY

★ · ★ · ★ · ★ · ★ · ★ · ★ · ★ · **1**

O	P	E	N
P	I	N	E
E	N	D	S
N	E	S	T

Clues:

1. To unlock
2. A tree
3. Finishes
4. Bird's home

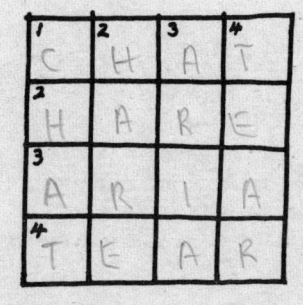

2

C	H	A	T
H	A	R	E
A	R	I	A
T	E	A	R

Clues:

1. Informal talk
2. Rabbit-like animal
3. Operatic melody
4. To rip

THIS WAY THAT WAY

★·★·★·★·★·★·★·★· **3**

	1	2	3	4
1	G	D	N	E
2	O	V	E	R
3	N	E	A	R
4	E	R	R	S

Clues:

1. Past
2. Above
3. Close by
4. Makes a mistake

4

	1	2	3	4
1	P	L	A	Y
2	L	U	R	E
3	A	R	E	A
4	Y	E	A	R

Clues:

1. To frolic
2. To tempt
3. A region
4. A period of time

THIS WAY THAT WAY

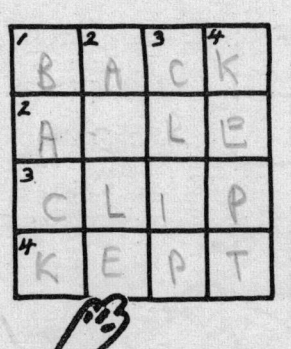

★ · ★ · ★ · ★ · ★ · ★ · ★ · **5**

	1	2	3	4
1	B	A	C	K
2	A	C	L	E
3		C	L	I	P
4	K	E	P	T

Clues:

1. The rear
2. A measure of land
3. To cut off
4. Retained

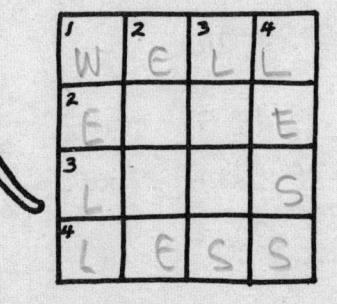

6

	1	2	3	4
1	W	E	L	L
2	E			E
3	L			S
4	L	E	S	S

Clues:

1. In good health
2. One of the Great Lakes
3. Moveable covers
4. Not so much

THIS WAY THAT WAY

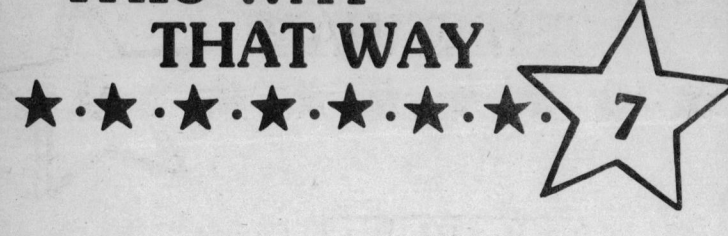

★ · ★ · ★ · ★ · ★ · ★ · ★ · **7**

Clues:

1. Drinks like a dog
2. Skilled
3. An appeal
4. Oceans

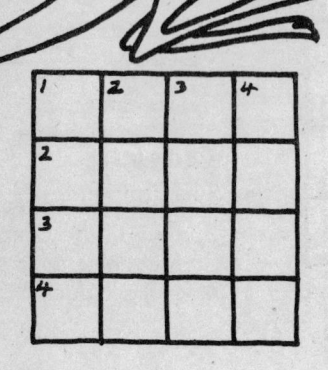

8

Clues:

1. Journey
2. Uncommon
3. A flower
4. A nuisance

THIS WAY THAT WAY

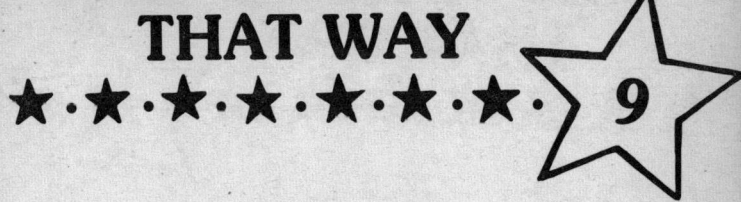

★ · ★ · ★ · ★ · ★ · ★ · ★ · **9**

Clues:

1. Farm implement
2. An only one
3. One time
4. Period of time

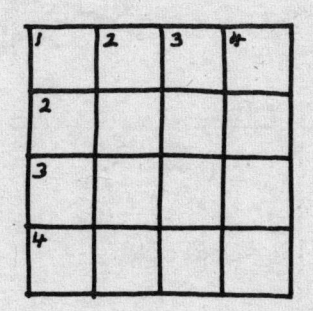

10

Clues:

1. Feeling joy
2. Part of the ear
3. Capable
4. Profound

THIS WAY THAT WAY

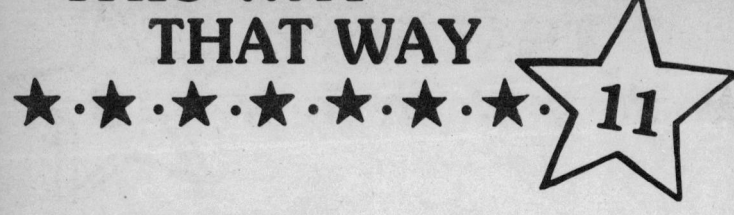

★·★·★·★·★·★·★· **11**

Clues:

1. Tears
2. Inactive
3. Plot
4. Dispatched

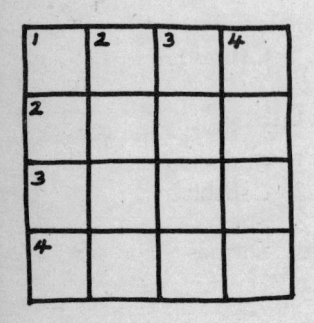

12

Clues:

1. A story
2. Prayer word
3. Allow temporary use
4. Completes

THIS WAY THAT WAY

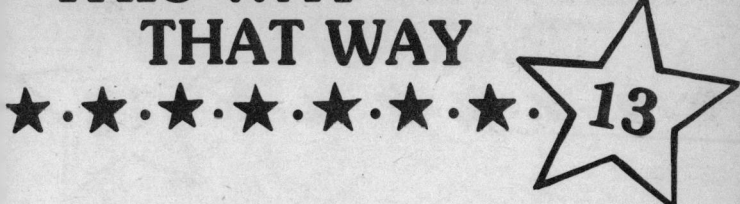

★ · ★ · ★ · ★ · ★ · ★ · ★ · **13**

Clues:

1. To give up
2. Unravel
3. Inactive
4. Part of the foot

14

Clues:

1. Containers
2. Capable
3. Shine
4. Stitches

THIS WAY THAT WAY

★ · ★ · ★ · ★ · ★ · ★ · ★ · **15**

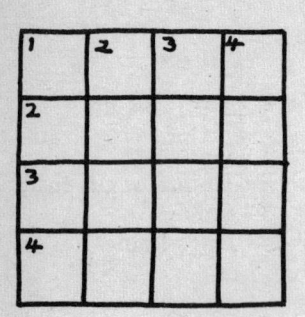

Clues:

1. A flower
2. Finished
3. A wise man
4. Makes a mistake

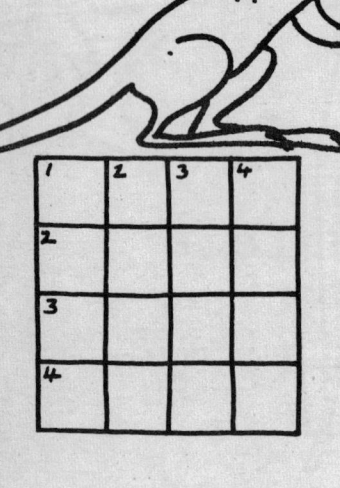

16

Clues:

1. Plaything
2. Musical instrument
3. Not short
4. Parts of the body

THIS WAY THAT WAY

17

Clues:

1. To rotate
2. To trim or cut away
3. Annoys
4. Bird's home

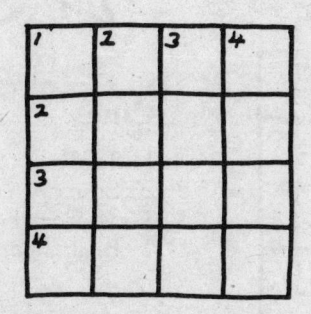

18

Clues:

1. To work the land
2. To entice
3. Spoken
4. Healthy

THIS WAY THAT WAY

★ ・ ★ ・ ★ ・ ★ ・ ★ ・ ★ ・ **19**

Clues:

1. Trout, for example
2. Thought
3. To vend
4. Hearty

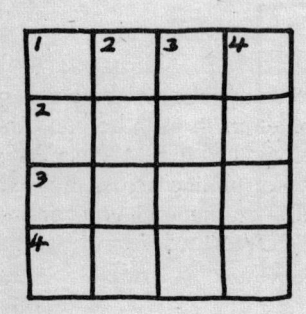

20

Clues:

1. Tardy
2. Sour
3. To clock
4. Biblical garden

BOX Words

Instructions:
Make 3-letter proper words by filling in the blank spaces between the top rows of letters in each box and the bottom rows. When you've filled in all the blanks, you should have a proper word running across the middle of each box. But be careful — sometimes you can make more than one proper "DOWN" word, and you have to choose the *right* one!

BOXWORDS
Boys' Names

★ · ★ · ★ · ★ · ★ · ★ · ★ · ★ · 1

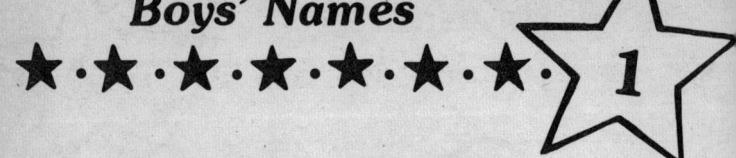

I	D	D	A
C	A	A	W
Y	D	Y	L

J	E	G	I
A	L		
W	M	G	N

I	T	E	F	O	H	U
Y	E	R	Y	D	M	E

A	T	D	I	M	U
E	E	G	P	T	E

E	B	D	D	A	J
G	D	G	Y	E	T

I	L	C	I	N	A
K	W	Y	P	G	T

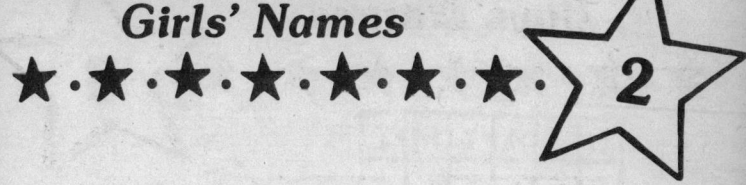

BOXWORDS
Girls' Names

★ · ★ · ★ · ★ · ★ · ★ · ★ · **2**

```
S K O O F     J A E K I
Y D D D N     T L M G N

  I N F E B I N A
  P P Y G G K W E

  I F O E B V I
  L G D M B N N

    A H D W
    D G Y G
```

How did you get to the doctor's so quickly?

Flu!

BOXWORDS
Sandwich Fillings

★ · ★ · ★ · ★ · ★ · ★ · ★ · 3

U	J	A	I	M	I
E	W	L	P	W	K

A	H	I	C	A	N
E	G	P	P	E	W

A	T	J	H	A	L
T	E	T	X	S	T

E	H	N	O
B	N	W	F

A	J	I	L
E	G	K	W

B	A	A
T	O	E

96

BOXWORDS
Fruit

★·★·★·★·★·★·★· 4

A	S	G	A	A	D
E	Y	M	K	M	E

O	J	I	C	I	F
I	G	K	R	N	T

E	P	I	C	E
M	T	P	P	W	D

A	J	C	A	T
E	T	N	E	Y

C	A	E	F	A	C	A
T	T	R	X	E	D	E

E	W	J	A	K
G	Y	R	E	G

Where do frogs hide their treasure?

In the riverbank, of course.

BOXWORDS
Musical Instruments

★·★·★·★·★·★·★· 5

I	O	J	I	J	I	N	S
Y	D	W	K	M	K	T	Y

O	I	H	A	F
F	L	E	E	Z

A	F	J	I	A
D	Y	G	P	H

A	H	J	I	F
E	D	G	K	X

I	W	E	O	B
E	T	K	D	X

I	F	V	I	W	A
Y	X	W	L	T	D

E	M	F	S	F	C
G	G	X	Y	N	Y

BOXWORDS
Colours

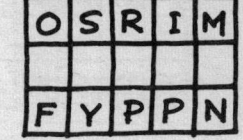

★ · ★ · ★ · ★ · ★ · ★ · 6

A	I	M	C	I	P	A
P	E	N	Y	L	T	E

O	N	I	A	F	N
T	T	K	E	U	T

B	O	F	I	E	H
B	E	D	N	G	R

E	B	O	S	B	O
E	T	D	Y	G	N

O	S	R	I	M
F	Y	P	P	N

BOXWORDS
Ice Cream Flavours

★ • ★ • ★ • ★ • ★ • ★ • 7

E	C	I	M	A	E	P
A	N	K	X	L	K	Y

I	P	A	I	J
P	N	E	L	T

B	A	E	I	E	W
W	M	T	N	G	T

A	A	W	S	W
E	T	X	Y	T

O	P	I	S
D	N	P	W

S	M	I	C	A
Y	T	P	T	T

100

BOXWORDS
Grocery List

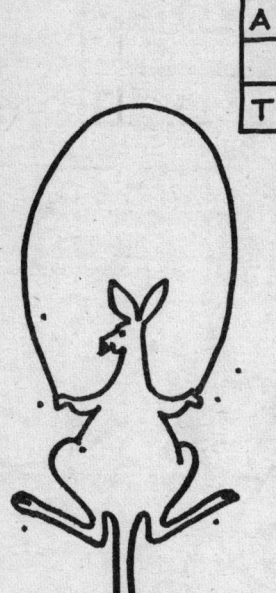

★ · ★ · ★ · ★ · ★ · ★ · ★ · 8

U	B	E	J	T
E	Y	O	M	Y

I	S	W	N	A	B
Y	Y	B	W	K	T

A	J	O	T	P	I
T	T	E	N	L	L

E	F	A	D	I
B	D	E	G	N

I	B	I	C	C
Y	G	E	D	N

ANAGRAMS

Instructions:
An anagram is made when you scramble the letters in one word to make a different word. Rearrange the letters in the words below to make new words. Think carefully — sometimes you can make more than one new word!

102

ANAGRAMS

★·★·★·★·★·★·★· **1**

1. EAST <u>SEAT</u>, <u>SATE</u> (TEAS written above)
2. WEST <u>STEW</u>, <u>WETS</u>
3. NORTH <u>THORN</u>
4. SOUTH <u>SHOUT</u>

2

1. OARS <u>SOAR</u>
2. HAWS <u>WASH</u>
3. PIER <u>RIPE</u>, <u>PERI</u>
4. CHIT <u>ITCH</u>

ANAGRAMS

★·★·★·★·★·★·★· 3

1. AUNT TUNA
2. ASCOT COATS, COAST
3. SLATE TALES, STALE
            TEALS, STEAL
4. ENLIST LISTEN, _____

4

1. LISA SAIL
2. ETHER THERE, _____
3. IDA AID
4. SMEAR MARES, _____

ANAGRAMS

★·★·★·★·★·★·★· ⭐5

1. HEART   <u>EARTH</u>
2. FARE   <u>FEAR</u>
3. BOAST _____
4. SPARED _____,

_____

⭐6

1. BOLT _____
2. HOST _____
3. DEALER _____
4. CENTRE _____

ANAGRAMS

★·★·★·★·★·★·★ 7

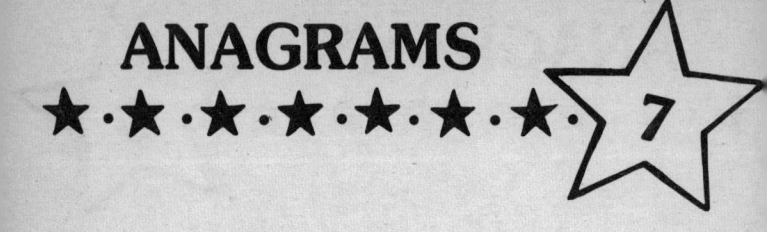

1. ARISE _ _ _ _ _
2. ALIGNS _ _ _ _ _ _
3. ANGER _ _ _ _ _
4. COWLS _ _ _ _ _

8

1. ENGLISH _ _ _ _ _ _ _
2. VOTES _ _ _ _ _
3. RACED _ _ _ _ _ , _ _ _ _ _
4. HEMS _ _ _ _

ANAGRAMS

★·★·★·★·★·★·★· 9

1. WEIRD _ _ _ _ _
2. PAGE _ _ _ _
3. HEAR _ _ _ _
4. DAD _ _ _

10

1. TRADE _ _ _ _ _ , _ _ _ _ _ ,
   _ _ _ _ _
2. SHEAR _ _ _ _ _ , _ _ _ _ _ ,
   _ _ _ _ _
3. GATES _ _ _ _ _ _
4. SATIN _ _ _ _ _

ANAGRAMS
★·★·★·★·★·★·★· 11

1. BAKES _ _ _ _ _
2. POLO _ _ _ _ , _ _ _ _
3. DARED _ _ _ _ _ , _ _ _ _ _
4. PORE _ _ _ _

Composers 12

1. HANDLE _ _ _ _ _ _
2. PHONIC _ _ _ _ _ _
3. BUTCHERS _ _ _ _ _ _ _ _
4. HANDY _ _ _ _ _

SOLUTIONS

CROSSWORDS

Crossword #1

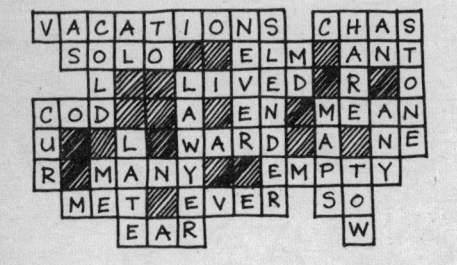

Crossword #2

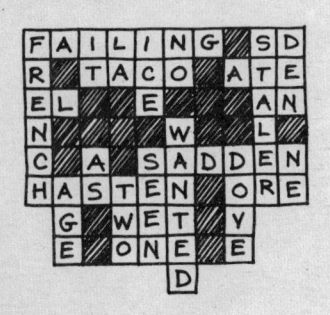

Crossword #3

Crossword #4

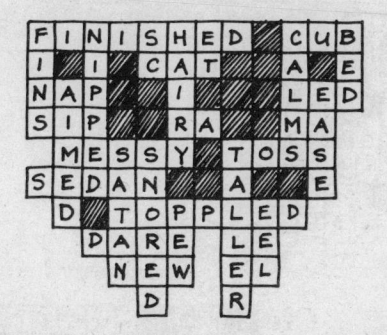

F	I	N	I	S	H	E	D		C	U	B
I		I		C	A	T			A		E
N	A	P			I			L	E	D	
S	I	P			R	A		M	A		
	M	E	S	S	Y		T	O	S	S	
S	E	D	A	N		A				E	
	D		T	O	P	P	L	E	D		
	D	A	R	E		L					
	N	E	W			E					
	D					R					

Crossword #5

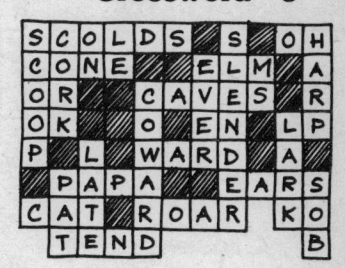

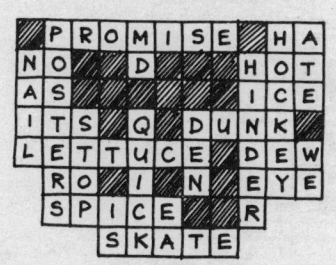

S	C	O	L	D	S		S		O	H	
C	O	N	E			E	L	M		A	
O	R			C	A	V	E	S		R	
O	K		O		E	N			L	P	
P		L		W	A	R	D		A		
	P	A	P	A			E	A	R	S	
C	A	T		R	O	A	R		K	O	B
	T	E	N	D							

Crossword #6

	P	R	O	M	I	S	E		H	A	
N	O		D				H	O	T		
A	S						I	C	E		
I	T	S		Q		D	U	N	K		
L	E	T	T	U	C	E		D	E	W	
	R	O		I		N		E	Y	E	
	S	P	I	C	E			R			
		S	K	A	T	E					

111

Crossword #7

```
              A
  COYOTE  FOX
OR    IL  ME
PA    INK IS
AMEND SPIT
LP ELM ONT
 SEVERAL E
 NE   NEED
 DRONES
  NOW
```

Crossword #8

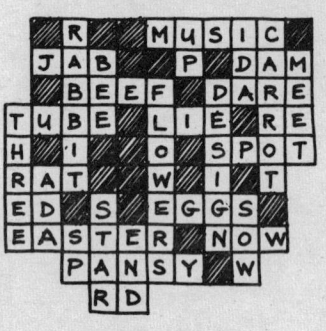

```
   R  MUSIC
  JAB  P DAM
  BEEF  DARE
TUBE  LIE RE
H  I   O SPOT
RAT  W  I T
RED S EGGS
EASTER  NOW
  PANSY  W
   RD
```

Crossword #9

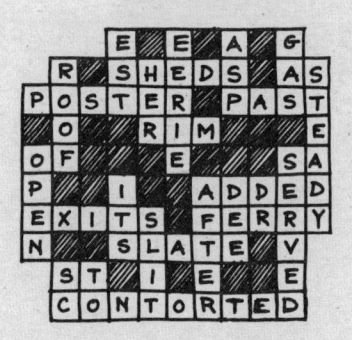

```
   E  E A  G
  R SHEDS AS
 POSTER PAST
  O  RIM  E
 OF  E   SA
P  I  ADDED
EXITS FERRY
N  SLATE V
ST  I  E E
CONTORTED
```

Crossword #10

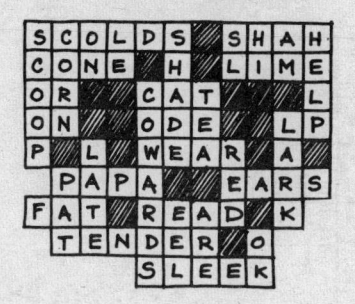

S	C	O	L	D	S			S	H	A	H
C	O	N	E		H			L	I	M	E
O	R			C	A	T					L
O	N		O	D	E			L	P		
P		L		W	E	A	R		A		
	P	A	P	A			E	A	R	S	
F	A	T		R	E	A	D		K		
	T	E	N	D	E	R		O			
			S	L	E	E	K				

Crossword #11

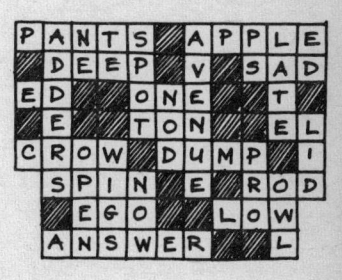

P	A	N	T	S		A	P	P	L	E
	D	E	E	P		V		S	A	D
E	D		O	N	E			T		
D				T	O	N		E	L	
C	R	O	W		D	U	M	P		I
	S	P	I	N		E		R	O	D
	E	G	O			L	O	W		L
A	N	S	W	E	R					L

Crossword #12

B	F									
E	V	E	R	Y	W	H	E	R	E	
A	A		E	E	L		G	O	O	S	E
T	H	R	E	E		F		G		P
	O		A			L				E
D	O	O	R		F	I	L		F	L	Y
	P	A	S	S		A	N	V	I	L
		T		A		L		E	V	E
	S	A	D	D	L	E			I	N
				S	A	I	L	I	N	G
				T					Y	

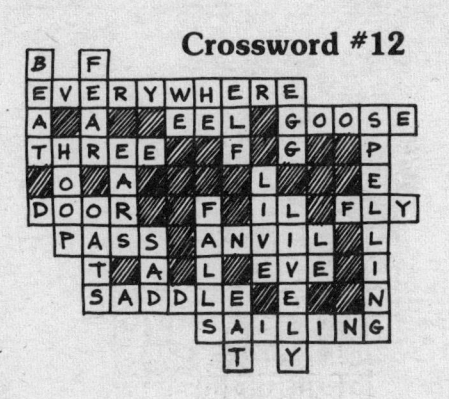

Crossword #13

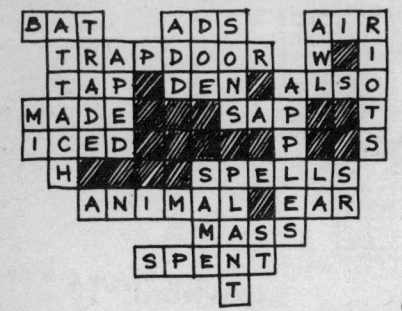

Crossword #14

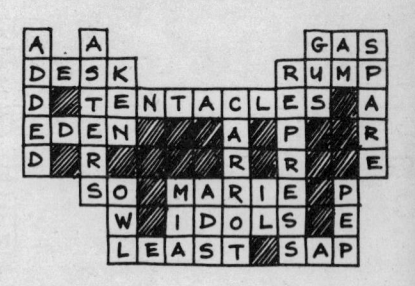

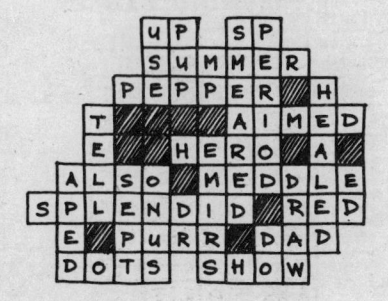

Crossword #15

Crossword #16

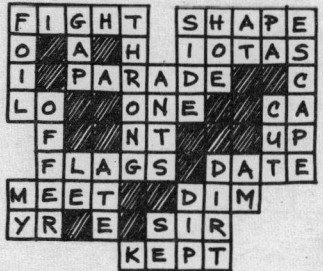

F	I	G	H	T		S	H	A	P	E
O		A		H		I	O	T	A	S
I		P	A	R	A	D	E			C
L	O			O	N	E		C	A	
	F			N	T			U	P	
	F	L	A	G	S		D	A	T	E
M	E	E	T			D	I	M		
Y	R		E		S	I	R			
			K	E	P	T				

Crossword #17

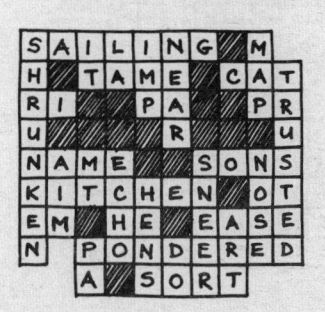

	R	A	B	B	I	T	S			
H	O	G			T	H	I	N	K	
O	D	E			E			I	M	P
A	P	E		O	V	E	R		A	N	D	Y
S	N	I	P		E			G		T
	T	R	E	E			H	A	D	H
	O	R				O			H	O	B	O
	N	A	G			N			M	N
			O	M	E	N				

Crossword #18

S	A	I	L	I	N	G		M		
H		T	A	M	E		C	A	T	
R	I			P	A			P	R	
U				R					U	
N	A	M	E			S	O	N	S	
K	I	T	C	H	E	N			O	T
E	M		H	E		E	A	S	E	
N		P	O	N	D	E	R	E	D	
	A		S	O	R	T				

Crossword #19

S	Y	R	U	P	■	A	F	T	E	R
U	■	■	■	A	S	S	■	■	■	O
N	B	■	■	N	I	P	■	■	■	D
D	I	S	H	E	S	■	T	A	K	E
A	R	I	A	■	■	R	A	D	I	O
Y	D	■	P	R	I	N	C	E	S	S
		U	P	■	T	■	K	■	S	
			Y	E	A	R	■	R	■	
			■	A	L	I	C	E	■	
			F	R	Y	■	O	D	D	

Crossword #20

		S	P	O	T				H	
	M	O	O	N	■	S	T	A	R	T
	U	N	D	E	R	■	O	N	■	I
I	S	■	■	■	O	■	■	T	E	N
T	I	■	■	P	A	■	■	I	■	■
	C	L	O	U	D	■	S	C	A	B
	■	O	■	N	■	■	O	S	L	O
	D	A	N	I	S	H	■	■	■	A
	■	D	■	S	■	E	A	R	■	T
			C	H	E	A	P	E	R	
						L	E	G		

Crossword #21

			B	E	E	T	L	E	S	■
	F	M	■	■	N	A	I	L	E	D
T	E	A	■	■	D	R	■	■	E	R
H	E	R	■	■	■	■	■	■	■	Y
I	■	K	A	N	G	A	R	O	O	■
N	E	E	D	■	E	■	■	■	A	T
K	A	T	E	■	A	S	■	A	R	E
■	R	■	S	T	R	E	A	M	S	■

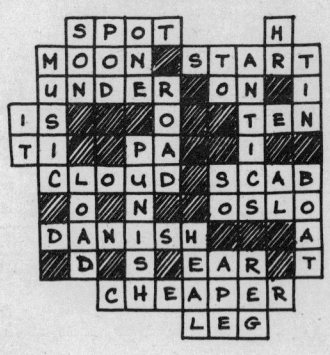

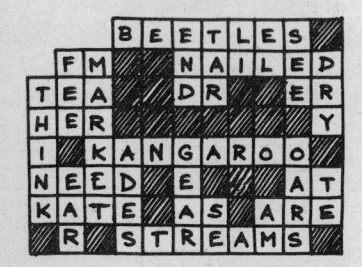

CENTRE LINES

★ · ★ · ★ · ★ · ★ · ★ · ★ · ★ · ★

Centre Line #1

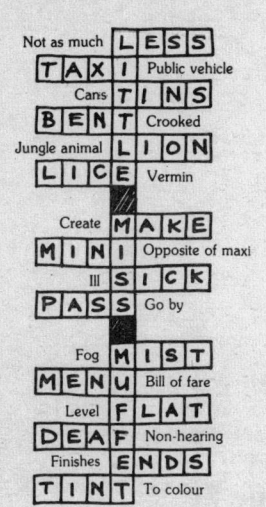

Not as much **LESS**
TAXI Public vehicle
Cans **TINS**
BENT Crooked
Jungle animal **LION**
LICE Vermin

Create **MAKE**
MINI Opposite of maxi
Ill **SICK**
PASS Go by

Fog **MIST**
MENU Bill of fare
Level **FLAT**
DEAF Non-hearing
Finishes **ENDS**
TINT To colour

Centre Line #2

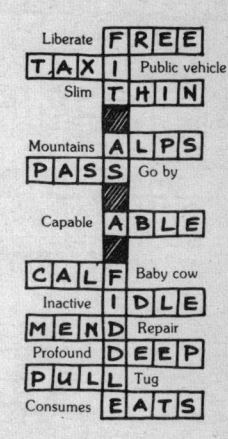

Liberate **FREE**
TAXI Public vehicle
Slim **THIN**

Mountains **ALPS**
PASS Go by

Capable **ABLE**

CALF Baby cow
Inactive **IDLE**
MEND Repair
Profound **DEEP**
PULL Tug
Consumes **EATS**

Centre Line #3

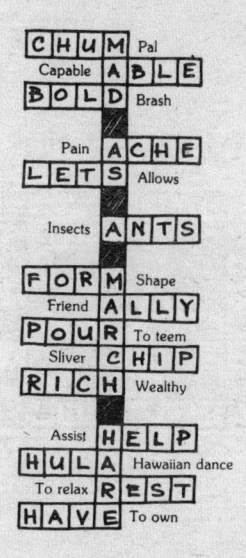

CHUM Pal
Capable **ABLE**
BOLD Brash

Pain **ACHE**
LETS Allows

Insects **ANTS**

FORM Shape
Friend **ALLY**
POUR To teem
Sliver **CHIP**
RICH Wealthy

Assist **HELP**
HULA Hawaiian dance
To relax **REST**
HAVE To own

Centre Line #4

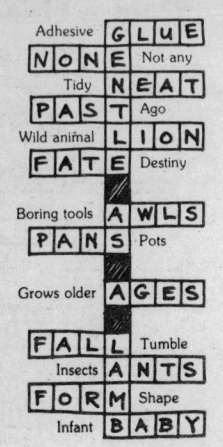

Adhesive	G L U E
N O N E	Not any
Tidy	N E A T
P A S T	Ago
Wild animal	L I O N
F A T E	Destiny

| Boring tools | A W L S |
| P A N S | Pots |

| Grows older | A G E S |

F A L L	Tumble
Insects	A N T S
F O R M	Shape
Infant	B A B Y

Centre Line #5

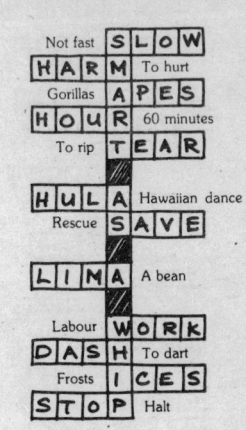

Not fast	S L O W
H A R M	To hurt
Gorillas	A P E S
H O U R	60 minutes
To rip	T E A R

| H U L A | Hawaiian dance |
| Rescue | S A V E |

| L I M A | A bean |

Labour	W O R K
D A S H	To dart
Frosts	I C E S
S T O P	Halt

Centre Line #6

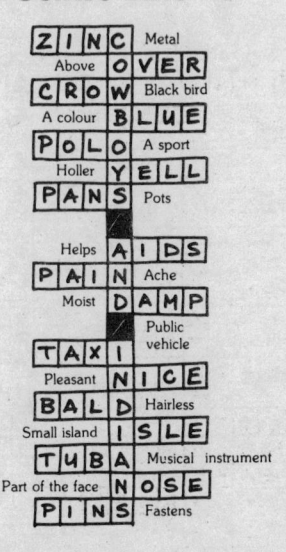

Z I N C	Metal
Above	O V E R
C R O W	Black bird
A colour	B L U E
P O L O	A sport
Holler	Y E L L
P A N S	Pots

Helps	A I D S
P A I N	Ache
Moist	D A M P
T A X I	Public vehicle
Pleasant	N I C E
B A L D	Hairless
Small island	I S L E
T U B A	Musical instrument
Part of the face	N O S E
P I N S	Fastens

Centre Line #7

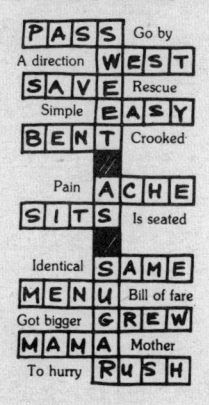

PASS — Go by
A direction — WEST
SAVE — Rescue
Simple — EASY
BENT — Crooked

Pain — ACHE
SITS — Is seated

Identical — SAME
MENU — Bill of fare
Got bigger — GREW
MAMA — Mother
To hurry — RUSH

Centre Line #8

Part of the face — CHIN
TEAR — Rip
Ventilates — AIRS
SUEZ — Famous canal
Shout — YELL

CUBA — Latin country
Remain — STAY

ASEA — On the ocean

Whip — LASH
FIDO — Dog's name
Above — OVER
NOON — Midday

Centre Line #9

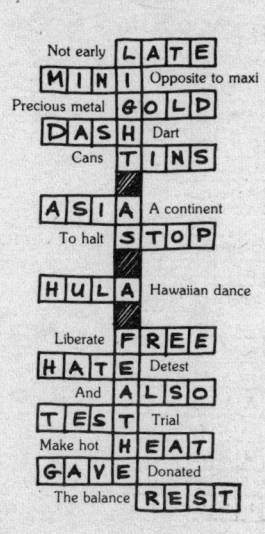

Not early — LATE
MINI — Opposite to maxi
Precious metal — GOLD
DASH — Dart
Cans — TINS

ASIA — A continent
To halt — STOP

HULA — Hawaiian dance

Liberate — FREE
HATE — Detest
And — ALSO
TEST — Trial
Make hot — HEAT
GAVE — Donated
The balance — REST

HIDDEN WORDS

Animals:
1. pig 2. zebra 3. cat 4. doe 5. hare 6. deer
7. jackass 8. fox 9. bat 10. rabbit 11. porcupine 12. mole
13. otter 14. leopard 15. ferret 16. ewe

Insects:
1. hornet 2. tsetse 3. ant 4. wasp 5. bee 6. fly

Birds:
1. wren 2. towhee 3. oriole 4. finch 5. starling 6. robin
7. thrush 8. parrot

Names:
1. Neil 2. Leon 3. Danny 4. Alice 5. Elise 6. Ethel
7. Sandra 8. Shannon 9. Tamara 10. Gene 11. Doug
12. Peter 13. Elsa 14. Arthur

Summer:
1. ants 2. tent 3. flower 4. camp 5. dive 6. lake 7. sand

Winter:
1. shovel 2. scarf 3. snowman 4. skates 5. sweater 6. mittens 7. rink

Vehicles:
1. trailer 2. bus 3. engine 4. cars 5. cart 6. wagon

Watercraft:
1. raft 2. boat 3. canoe 4. yacht 5. ship 6. ferry 7. skiff

Fires:
1. siren 2. water 3. heat 4. escape 5. ladder 6. hook 7. helmet

Carpentry:
1. saw 2. drill 3. nail 4. axe 5. ladders 6. plane 7. shavings

Flavours:
1. caramel 2. vanilla 3. almond 4. lemon 5. lime 6. mint 7. licorice

Desserts:
1. pies 2. cake 3. tart 4. peach 5. ice cream 6. custard 7. jello

Relatives:
1. aunt 2. uncle 3. sister 4. niece 5. father 6. brother 7. mother

Vegetables:
1. carrot 2. onion 3. tomato 4. turnip 5. leek 6. beet 7. peas

Back to school:
1. teacher 2. lesson 3. pupil 4. chalk 5. desk 6. eraser 7. paper

Ailments:
1. measles 2. mumps 3. cold 4. flu 5. virus 6. headache 7. earache

SECRET CODES

★ · ★ · ★ · ★ · ★ · ★ · ★ · ★ · ★

Colours:
orange, yellow, scarlet, purple, green

Pets:
kitten, budgie, gerbil, turtle, hamster

Languages:
Spanish, Italian, Hebrew, French, Greek

Animals:
cat, bear, deer, camel, seal, tiger

Birds:
raven, oriole, grouse, turkey, parrot, cuckoo

Swimming creatures:
cod, trout, shrimp, perch, bass, smelt

Pictures:
canvas, paint, frame, glass, wire

Drawing supplies:
pencil, crayon, chalk, charcoal, pastels

Tools:
hammer, chisel, wrench, file, pliers

Winter:
snowman, sleet, drifts, freeze, icicle

Composers:
Mozart, Schubert, Brahms, Chopin, Dussek

THIS WAY THAT WAY

★ · ★ · ★ · ★ · ★ · ★ · ★ · ★ · ★

#1

O	P	E	N
P	I	N	E
E	N	D	S
N	E	S	T

#2

C	H	A	T
H	A	R	E
A	R	I	A
T	E	A	R

#3

G	O	N	E
O	V	E	R
N	E	A	R
E	R	R	S

#4

P	L	A	Y
L	U	R	E
A	R	E	A
Y	E	A	R

#5

B	A	C	K
A	C	R	E
C	R	O	P
K	E	P	T

#6

W	E	L	L
E	R	I	E
L	I	D	S
L	E	S	S

#7

L	A	P	S
A	B	L	E
P	L	E	A
S	E	A	S

#8

T	R	I	P
R	A	R	E
I	R	I	S
P	E	S	T

#9

P	L	O	W
L	O	N	E
O	N	C	E
W	E	E	K

#10

G	L	A	D
L	O	B	E
A	B	L	E
D	E	E	P

#11
```
R I P S
I D L E
P L A N
S E N T
```

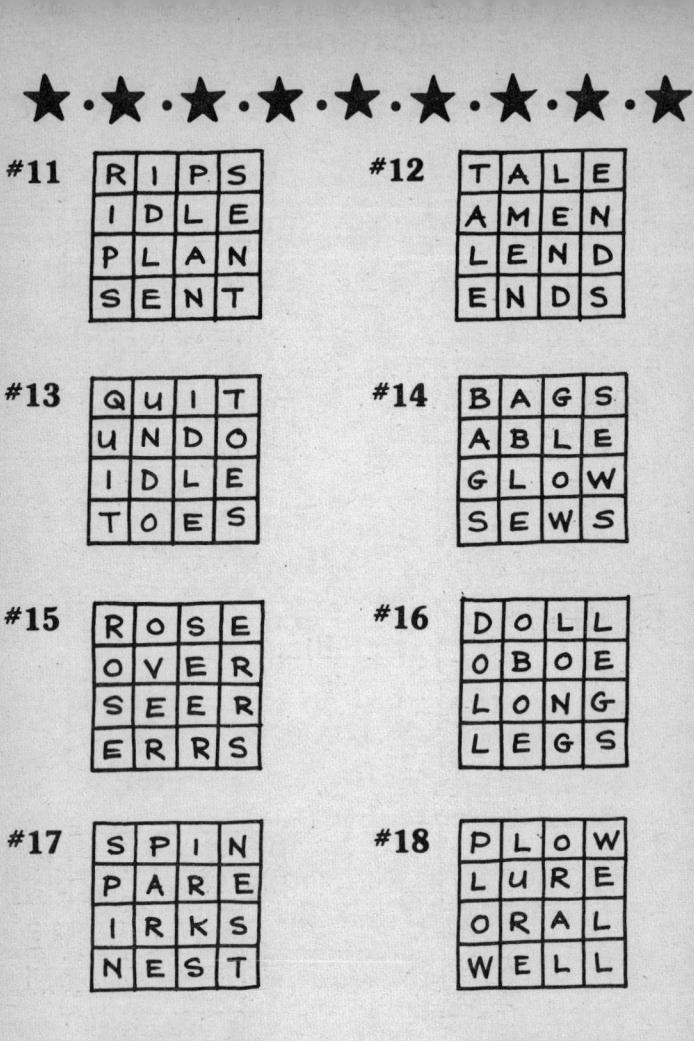

#12
```
T A L E
A M E N
L E N D
E N D S
```

#13
```
Q U I T
U N D O
I D L E
T O E S
```

#14
```
B A G S
A B L E
G L O W
S E W S
```

#15
```
R O S E
O V E R
S E E R
E R R S
```

#16
```
D O L L
O B O E
L O N G
L E G S
```

#17
```
S P I N
P A R E
I R K S
N E S T
```

#18
```
P L O W
L U R E
O R A L
W E L L
```

#19
```
F I S H
I D E A
S E L L
H A L E
```

#20
```
L A T E
A C I D
T I M E
E D E N
```

BOXWORDS

★ · ★ · ★ · ★ · ★ · ★ · ★ · ★ · ★

Boys' Names

| I D D A |
| C A R L |
| Y D Y L |

| J E G I |
| A L A N |
| W M G N |

| I T E F O H U |
| C H A R L E S |
| Y E R Y D M E |

| A T D I M U |
| T H O M A S |
| E E G P T E |

| E B D D A J |
| G E O R G E |
| G D G Y E T |

| I L C I N A |
| N O R M A N |
| K W Y P G T |

Girls' Names

| S K O O F |
| H I L D A |
| Y D D D N |

| J A E K I |
| E L L E N |
| T L M G N |

| I N F E B I N A |
| M A R G A R E T |
| P P Y G G K W E |

| I F O E B V I |
| L I L L I A N |
| L G D M B N N |

| A H D W |
| D O R A |
| D G Y G |

Sandwich Fillings

| U J A I M I |
| S A L M O N |
| E W L P W K |

| A H I C A N |
| T O M A T O |
| E G P P E W |

| A T J H A L |
| C H E E S E |
| T E T X S T |

| E H N O |
| B E E F |
| B N W F |

| A J I L |
| T U N A |
| E G K W |

| B A A |
| E G G |
| T O E |

Fruit

| A S G A A D |
| C H E R R Y |
| E Y M K M E |

| O J I C I F |
| B A N A N A |
| I G K R N T |

| E P I C E |
| L E M O N |
| M T P W D |

| A J C A T |
| P E A C H |
| E T N E Y |

| C A E F A C A |
| A P R I C O T |
| T T R X E D E |

| E W J A K |
| G R A P E |
| G Y R E G |

Musical Instruments

I	O	J	I	J	I	N	S
C	L	A	R	I	N	E	T
Y	D	W	K	M	K	T	Y

O	I	H	A	F
F	L	U	T	E
F	L	E	E	Z

A	F	J	I	A
D	R	U	M	S
D	Y	G	P	H

A	H	J	I	F
P	I	A	N	O
E	D	G	K	X

I	W	E	O	B
C	E	L	L	O
E	T	K	D	X

I	F	V	I	W	A
V	I	O	L	I	N
Y	X	W	L	T	D

E	M	F	S	F	C
G	U	I	T	A	R
G	G	X	Y	N	Y

Colours

A	I	M	C	I	P	A
S	C	A	R	L	E	T
P	E	N	Y	L	T	E

O	N	I	A	F	N
P	U	R	P	L	E
T	T	K	E	U	T

B	O	F	I	E	H
O	R	A	N	G	E
B	E	D	N	G	R

E	B	O	S	B	O
Y	E	L	L	O	W
E	T	D	Y	G	N

O	S	R	I	M
F	L	A	M	E
F	Y	P	P	N

Ice Cream Flavours

E	C	I	M	A	E	P
V	A	N	I	L	L	A
A	N	K	X	L	K	Y

I	P	A	I	J
M	A	P	L	E
P	N	E	L	T

B	A	E	I	E	W
O	R	A	N	G	E
W	M	T	N	G	T

A	A	W	S	W
G	R	A	P	E
E	T	X	Y	T

O	P	I	S
L	I	M	E
D	N	P	W

S	M	I	C	A
L	E	M	O	N
Y	T	P	T	T

Grocery List

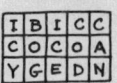

U	B	E	J	T
S	U	G	A	R
E	Y	O	M	Y

I	S	W	N	A	B
C	H	E	E	S	E
Y	Y	B	W	K	T

A	J	O	T	P	I
C	E	R	E	A	L
T	T	E	N	L	L

E	F	A	D	I
B	A	C	O	N
B	D	E	G	N

I	B	I	C	C
C	O	C	O	A
Y	G	E	D	N

ANAGRAMS

★ · ★ · ★ · ★ · ★ · ★ · ★ · ★ · ★

Anagrams #1:
1. teas or seat 2. stew or wets 3. thorn 4. shout

Angrams #2:
1. soar 2. wash 3. ripe 4. itch

Anagrams #3:
1. tuna 2. coats or coast 3. steal, least, stale or tales 4. listen or silent

Anagrams #4:
1. sail 2. three or there 3. aid 4. mares or reams

Anagrams #5:
1. earth 2. fear 3. boats 4. spread or drapes

Anagrams #6:
1. blot 2. shot 3. leader 4. recent

Anagrams #7:
1. raise 2. signal 3. range 4. scowl

Anagrams #8:
1. shingle 2. stove 3. cared or cedar 4. mesh

Anagrams #9:
1. wider 2. gape 3. hare 4. add

Anagrams #10:
1. tread, rated or dater 2. share, hears or hares 3. stage 4. stain

Anagrams #11:
1. beaks 2. pool or loop 3. dread or adder 4. rope

Anagrams #12:
1. Handel 2. Chopin 3. Schubert 4. Haydn

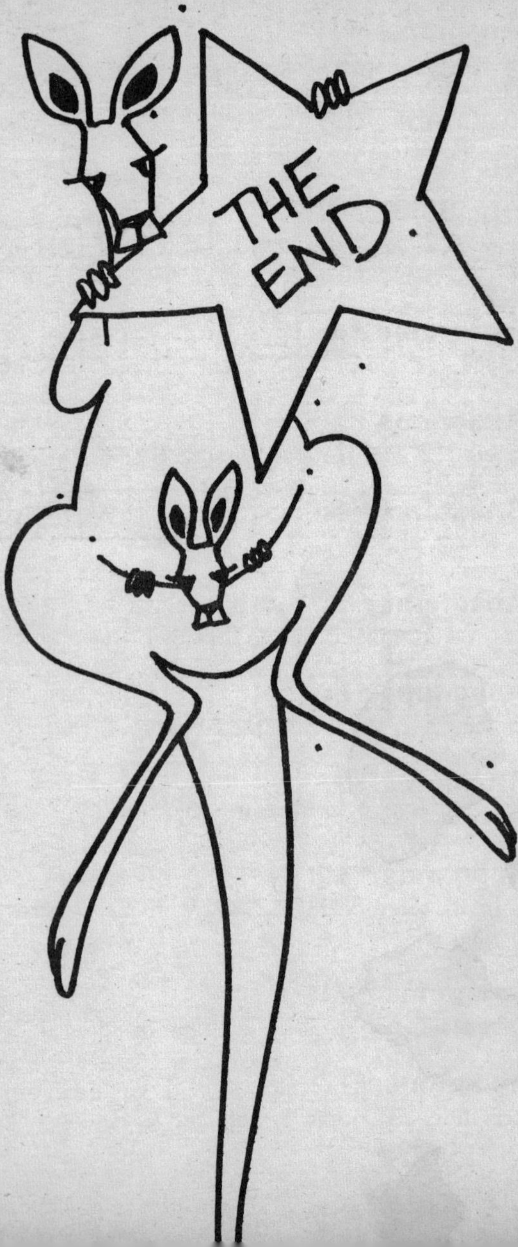
THE
END